Herein Is Love - Capacity to Live

Herein Is Love –
Capacity to Live

AND OTHER THINGS I LEARNED
IN SPECIAL ED CLASS

Nancy Caughron

I use the King James Version of the *The Holy Bible*, bound with three other books of scripture - the *Book of Mormon*, *Doctrine and Covenants*, and *Pearl of Great Price*. This Quadruple Combination of scriptures is published by The Church of Jesus Christ of Latter-day Saints, Salt Lake City, Utah 1989. All references to scripture are from this book. All references to the Topical Guide, Index, or Bible Dictionary are found in this book. Some verses of the Bible have a translation by Joseph Smith, which are also included.

Priesthood blessings refer to an ordinance wherein a blessing of comfort or healing is requested from a man who bears the Priesthood of God. He, and usually a companion who also bears the Priesthood, lay hands upon your head and offer a blessing, speaking what inspiration comes to their mind and heart from the Lord, for the benefit of the person seeking a blessing.

© 2018 Nancy Caughron
All rights reserved.

ISBN-13: 9781984265494
ISBN-10: 1984265490
Library of Congress Control Number: 2018902144
CreateSpace Independent Publishing Platform
North Charleston, South Carolina

For the Sheep in My Fold . . . And His
And for ALL My Fellow Travelers

Preface

WHEN I MADE MY MONUMENTAL Leap of Faith, and decided to trust - and love - my Father in Heaven, I tested Him. The test was this question:

Where is the love?

I was holding God accountable for His behavior.

It may sound blasphemous to some people. I was hoping and mostly expecting to find love from Him - - but I had taken a HUGE risk in my Leap of Faith and for a long time I continued that Leap day-to-day with trembling and trepidation. Sometimes the Leap was desperate and fear-filled. I struggled to live in those times.

God did not seem to mind. I think He was simply glad, and grateful, that I was leaping in the first place.

I was looking for evidence of the integrity of His heart and I found it. Every time.

I no longer test Him. He has proven Himself faithful in all things. I have done this for so many years that now I see the love automatically. It tickles me. It delights me. I often tell Him how great He is for the evidences I find.

John said, *Herein is love . . . that he loved us.*[1]

Along the way to learning this marvelous Truth about Godly Love, I learned what it *means.* The fruit of Godly Love is this - Capacity to Live. Through anything.

Table of Contents

Happy Birthday, Teacher!

MANY YEARS AGO WHEN WE lived in Washington, Michelle (my oldest) worked in a junior high school as a teacher's aide in a special education class. She loved her job. One of the things taught in the class was how to take the city bus and how to behave in public - they took many short trips so they could gain this valuable skill.

Toward the end of the school year Michelle came home full of that day's events. The school had a special assembly in the auditorium. All the students were assembled - no one knew why they were there; it was not a scheduled assembly.

It was announced to all the students that this was a special award assembly for the special education class in their school. A representative of the city transit company was there that day to honor the special education class of their school with a special award. He made it clear that this class of students had brought honor to the school and every student in it. He explained how well they had behaved and how excellent they had become in riding the bus and representing their school.

The special education class received a standing ovation from the rest of the school.

This story has stayed with me and still brings tears to my eyes when I think of it.

For three years I have served as the Young Women's president of the state hospital branch of my church in Provo. (I have had excellent counselors without whom I could not function.) The girls on the unit are from 12 to 18 years old. I love my girls.

Some time ago a few of the girls started talking about school and how they were treated and the names they were called. It turned out each had been in a special ed class in their various schools. They had been ridiculed and mocked because they were special ed students. They were called dumb and stupid and many other derogatory names. Their feelings had been hurt. Then they said there were lots of reasons for a student to be placed in a special ed class. A student might have behavior problems or couldn't concentrate or a medication could make it difficult to process information - a wide variety of problems could cause a student to be placed in special ed.

The girls talked about how much they loved being in a special ed class because they loved their teachers. It was poignant and beautiful to hear. These girls were from all over the state, but their teachers seemed to have the same attributes. Their teachers were patient; students could ask questions again and again and the teacher would explain in different ways until they understood. The teacher didn't get mad when they didn't understand. There was no ridicule or mockery. Students were encouraged and loved. They received individual attention. They were praised. The teacher had faith in them. It was safe to make a mistake.

These special ed teachers looked beyond limitations and saw potential. They patiently, carefully, lovingly, firmly, and forgivingly understood and worked with the limitations - and taught to the potential.

I have spent my life in a special ed class. Some things have been incredibly hard for me to learn; many things I am still working on. I admit that I don't always do my homework and I too often fail the tests. I am a slow learner sometimes. I am too often foolish. I wonder about myself often, and fear what might be really true about me. It can be hard to shake off discouragement when the tone of our society is clever ridicule and mockery. It takes courage to try - mistakes can be embarrassing - even shameful.

Here is the good news - I have a GREAT teacher!

I can ask questions any time. He is patient and considerate. He does not use mockery or ridicule - rather, He encourages even as He corrects. He forgives me when I don't do my homework - reminding me that it will just take longer for me to learn the lesson. He tells me the only way I will fail is if I quit. If I don't come to class, He seeks me out.

Sometimes I am unruly in class; I even cause a disturbance for other students. He takes me aside and helps me see my errors and shows me how I can do better. It is impossible to exaggerate the perfection of His teachings or His methods.

He sees past my limitations and teaches to my potential. His class is a safe place.

This Earth is a Special Ed class for each of us.

Jesus Christ is our teacher. He came to Earth and attended a Special Ed class of His own - specifically tailored to His complete *absence* of limitations. There has never been nor will ever be another like it. Only He could have endured the lessons, the homework, the graduation exam in *that* school! He is uniquely qualified to understand how and what to teach us. He seeks us out and joyfully receives us when we come to Him - no matter how flawed we may be!

I believe that if we show up for class and do our best, each of us will attend an awards assembly in our honor. The rest of the students in this mortal school will rise in appreciation when we see how well each of us learned to ride the bus - our obvious limitations will only make the accomplishment more precious.

School is not easy for me, but Oh! I love my Teacher! He is teaching me how to ride this bus that I am on - and how to behave while I am doing it.

So I rise and I kneel in honor, respect and inexpressible gratitude to the One student who rode this bus perfectly. He is my companion on *my* bus, my mentor and my Savior. He paid the fare so I could ride: free to ride and free to get off when I get home.

My Christmas gift to you is that I thank you for your successes in *your* bus ride. I am grateful to you for staying on the bus, for not giving up. Thank you for bringing honor to me and our school. I have faith in your potential beyond your limitations. And I trust the ability of your Teacher to bring you home!

See you at your Assembly!

The Best And The Most

I THINK MY WORST CHRISTMAS ever was in 1981. I was a new single parent with six children in a new town in a new state. I had no job and no car. That year had brought tremendous trauma to my family and it wasn't over. Things would get worse. With no income I could purchase nothing for my children. It was a terrible time for us.

Then the Welcome Wagon lady came to our door. She saw our distress and gave me the best present I could have. She insisted on taking me shopping to buy stocking stuffers for my children. She told me to get whatever it was that they traditionally expected to have in their stockings Christmas morning. For a little while the nightmare receded. It was an amazingly thoughtful thing for her to do - I would say inspired. She gave me the gift of having something to give.

This September I received a phone call at work from one of my children. He told me his doctor had just confirmed that he had cancer. I was very rational on the phone. When our discussion was over, I turned to my computer to continue working. I worked for about five minutes. Then the reaction set in.

The only thing I could think of was that I needed to get a blessing. This was something I couldn't fix. I sought a friend at work whose husband has the priesthood - I wanted to see if he would give me a blessing. I found her in my boss' office. He gestured for me to come in, saw my face, and asked what was wrong. I blurted out, "I just found out my son has cancer and I need a blessing." A few minutes later he and two other priesthood holders in our department gave me a blessing.

I was not told that the cancer would go away. I was not told that my son would be made well, or some other great miracle of that type would occur. I was not told that we would not be required to drink from this cup.

I *was* told that I had had many hard trials. It brought tears to my eyes. I thought, *My Father noticed!* Then I was told that I would be able to draw on the strength those trials had given me. And I was stunned. I saw that the trials were a gift - I had been prepared for this new situation. My Father had given me what I needed to be able to drink from this cup, too.

He gave me the gift of having strength to give my son and his family. The gift of having something to give.

Gifts are symbols of the love we have for others. The great desire is to give the best and the most that we can. We stretch our resources because no matter what we do - the gift is still only a symbol. Within our resources, we look for the gifts that say *I see you. I notice you. This is for you because I love you.* I have never heard anyone say, "I love Bill (or Susie) so much! What is the least I can give them?"

We will give until it hurts.

I have been thinking about the greatest Giver of gifts - my Father in Heaven. His gifts are wonderful - full of Wonder. He sometimes gives in unique and unexpected ways. I have learned to be still and attend or I may miss the gift altogether. I may even misunderstand it.

Remember that our Savior came to this earth so that He may know how to succor us in our infirmities? His trials are a gift to us. He knows by experience what we need. His experience gave Him what we need for Him to give us.

I realize that one of the great gifts my Savior has given me is endurance. He surely has blessed me to be able to endure. He has also shown me what endurance is. It is singularly significant that when He was crucified - and still enduring the Atonement - He did not say *This is over. I am done suffering for these people. I quit!*

I love that the scriptures record what He said: *It is finished.* He endured until the trial was completed. Not only that - and equally significant - He endured in love. He began and ended His life in unwavering love for us and for His Father.

He still endures in love. He is not bitter when His love for us is unreturned. He is not bitter because His earthly life was so filled with tribulation and suffering. He continues to endure in love for His Father, for me, and for you.

My Father and my Savior have taught me everything about gifts and giving. Some trials can not be removed - it is then that we strengthen others to help them endure, looking for the understanding our own lives have given us (by precious experience) so that we may know how to succor them. We seek to endure our own trials in love so we are not found wanting when we are needed.

We find a remarkable compassion and understanding for our Father and our Savior when we do this. We enter into fellowship with them. We begin to be able to give our Best and our Most.

So, in all the imperfect giving I do and with all the desire of my heart to give perfectly - this Truth is my something to give - my Best and Most:

> You have a Father in Heaven. He is your true Father; you are His child. He has prepared every needful and wantful thing for you. He has embodied His love for you in His Son, Jesus Christ, and given Him to you for your very own gift. Pay attention to that gift. Do not misunderstand it. You came here with desire to be like the Gift you were given - even Jesus Christ. Love Him. Know Him. Turn to Him. Notice the gifts you are given that make you like Him - your experiences. Endure them as He did - and does. Endure in love. Let them give you the gift of having something to give.

My gratitude to all of you who daily give your Best and Most.

My endless gratitude to my Father for giving me his Best and Most: my own Savior.

Promise We Can Come Home!

WHEN WE HEARD OUR FATHER'S plan the first time, we wanted reassurance that we would be coming back Home.

When we said *Goodbye* to our grandparents and parents - they had to leave and come to earth before us - we asked again to hear the promise that they would be coming back home. Our children said *Goodbye* to us when we came, and relied again on our Father's promise that we would return.

When it was our turn to come to earth it took faith to leave home - and again we said, *Father, tell me again. You promise that this is temporary? You promise we can come home?*

And He did. So we left.

We don't know how to understand what we call death in this life. We have forgotten that we have had this separation before, when we lived at Home with our Father in Heaven and all our heavenly family. We left Home and family and dearly beloved Parents for this mortal education. It took faith. It took a Godly promise.

He said, *This is not forever. You will come Home. I promise.*

So we, in this life with the forgetfulness of our Heavenly Home, do not remember that we blessed our Father for giving us the promise we call death.

How precious death is to Father's children! He is keeping His promise to us. The separation is not forever! The hearts of our spirits yearn to be Home when our education and experience in mortal life is done. And saying *Goodbye* is for us here, even as it was for us when we were Home, only temporary. We can count on it.

He promised we could all go Home.

It is my testimony to you that earthly death is the only way that this life makes any sense. It is a necessary and perfect part of a perfect plan - a plan that blesses us with its grace and compassion. A plan of understanding love. Parting is sorrowful, but it is not wrong. Separation brings grief, but it is not bad. There is a vital difference between wrong and sorrow, between bad and grief. There are many things that are right and hard at the same time. Ask the Savior. He knows about grief, sorrow, and hard, right things that must be done. And He promises to help us with our sorrows, griefs, separations, and hard, right things that we must do.

Please trust this truth: Heavenly Father keeps His promises. He promised that we can go home, that our separation does not have to be forever. We trusted Him. Death is the promise that we counted on, that gave us the courage to come here in the first place. Bless His heart, He keeps His promises.

Careful in Love - Bold in Declaration

AT THE END OF THE movie *Dances With Wolves*, Wind In His Hair mounts his horse and rides to the top of a cliff that overlooks the trail of his friend's departure. He then shouts his goodbye to Dances With Wolves,

"Dances With Wolves. I am Wind In His Hair. Do you see that I am your friend? Can you see that you will always be my friend?

"Dances With Wolves.

"Dances With Wolves.

"Dances With Wolves . . . "

This scene is the reason I own the DVD of this movie; I will sometimes put in the DVD only to watch this scene. This declaration of love is for me the entire intent of the movie.

This Christmas season the words **Careful in Love, Bold in Declaration** have been echoing in my mind and heart. These words are about my Father and my Savior and me - and you.

There are images that have come to my mind; they seem random and disconnected. First, I thought of the Winter Quarters Temple, with all its focused detail on the pioneers who sacrificed, suffered, and died there. The temple itself is a bold declaration of love in its entirety and its detail. People who were rejected and driven out, throw-away people of the society of their times who must have felt forsaken by humanity, were noticed in every point of their lives and more than a century later the minutia of their lives is displayed - a careful and bold declaration of love by their God.

In my mind I see Moroni revealed to all the world, all over the world; his statue outlined in the sky for all to see: a bold proclamation of God's love for a man who lived hidden and hiding, pursued for hate and destruction, now majestically claimed as God's treasured friend.

My mind then turns inward, to the guarded places of my heart - the places of my piercing wounds, my poignant hopes, my penetrating fears - places of exquisite sorrow. I do not attend these places except in apprehensive, trembling glance and hasty retreat. My Savior is not so tenuous. He carefully knows the delicate and tender details of my wounds and ministers to them in patience and compassion, without haste to leave or shame in attending. How bold and careful He is in my heart!

I think of all the preparation of nesting that accompanied the anticipated arrival of a new child to my home. I loved having babies. I repeated this nesting whenever we moved - we were always settled into our home in a day; my children's rooms were done by bedtime. I wanted them to know this was home and they belonged; I wanted them to know they mattered most of all.

The nesting of this world for us is perfect and complete in all its detail. The Universe itself is a bold declaration of love and attendance to love. All for us!

Here is the tender message I have received this year. There is no more careful attention or bold declaration of love for me than the tiny babe lying in a manger in Bethlehem. This infant is the healing of wounds and surcease of fears. He is hope realized and the oil of joy for mourning. He is beauty for ashes.

The intent of His existence is careful and bold declaration of love - the Atonement. He calls me by name and declares that He is my Friend. He eternally pleads that I will be His friend. This declaration is the boldest shout of love and love's most careful whisper. And, like Wind In His Hair to Dances With Wolves, He never ceases to call my name.

Black Holes and The Physics of Freedom

BLACK HOLES ARE VORACIOUS, GREEDY phenomena in our Universe. Named for their lack of light, any particle that wanders close to their Event Horizon - - their gravitational boundary or point of no return - - is sucked into the hole, never to be released.

Points of light - photons - considered the fastest particles in existence - can not move fast enough to escape a Black Hole once they are caught. Hence the term Black Hole - having powerful properties of attraction, a Black Hole emits no light at all.

Consider that Lucifer - Prince of Darkness - is the Black Hole in our Universe. Consider as well that each of us, having been born with the Light of Christ, is a photon or point of light in our Universe.

We have been given the power to choose where we go. We may choose to be disciples of Christ, to journey freely in the Light of day. As such, we are always free to stay or leave, as we desire.

Or we may be followers after Lucifer, who entices us to wander into his twilight sphere of influence until, with ever-increasing gravity, his powerful properties of attraction and addiction carry us within his event horizon - his point of no return, as he would have us believe. The trap is sprung and we are caught in the Dark.

Our efforts to remove ourselves from this prison avail us nothing. Hopeless, helpless, dismayed, and despairing - there is no way out.

Enter the Savior and His Atonement. He alone entered the endless night (no moon or stars there!), the domain of the Prince of Darkness, the terrible Black Hole of Souls – and returned. He conquered the Dark and overcame the power of the event horizon.

Lucifer's rule over darkness fell in that moment.

The Light of Souls, the Author of Freedom, the Way of Rescue, Jesus Christ proved He is Master over all – Day *and* Night.

Such is the power of the Sacrifice of the Son of God. He took His Light across the event horizon of sin into the dark prison of souls, Lucifer's Black Hole and realm of night, and by the Majesty of His Light and Love for us He opened doors and forged a path to Freedom.

The path is called Repentance. It is sacred and bought with Holy Light. By that Light shackles fall, darkness is banished, and our brilliant Light re-emerges.

Essential Celestial Physics.

Christmas Hope

2007 WAS A YEAR THAT brought many changes to my family – and to my life. In June I moved in with my son, who was still going through a divorce and struggling with all the attendant heartaches, changes, uncertainties and fears. There had been other equally distressing events in my family and all these experiences brought me to an odd place.

During that Christmas season I wondered about hope. It has been one of the most difficult commandments for me to embrace. I sort of glance over it with my eyes – it is much easier for me to focus on faith and charity. So I have sort of skipped the middle of faith, hope, and charity.

That Christmas I was ready for hope (although I didn't know it). It was unexpected and began quietly and simply with a question – or a wonder. I found myself thinking that it was interesting that Christ, the hope of the world, came into the world as helpless and vulnerable as a newborn babe. The hope of the world was an *infant*.

I pursued the wonder. I thought, *We are commanded to have hope. Christ is our hope – we are to have hope in Christ. I have learned that we are given no commandment that is not Godly in its truth and principle. So does God hope? If we are to be more like Him, and Father's entire purpose is to help us be like Him – then Hope must be a Godly attribute. Hmmm . . . . I think I'm onto something here.*

And I was.

I was in anguish of spirit over the trials some of my children were facing. I knew that my only hope for my children rested in the Savior. They needed Him. My ability to have hope for my children rested in the Savior and His Atonement, His compassion, His certain succor in our infirmities. I couldn't heal their wounds (I couldn't heal my own . . . .).

I depended on Jesus Christ, the infant and mortal Son of God, to give my children what I could not. Without Him, my hope for them was lost. It couldn't even begin.

Well, I told you that so I can tell you this.

Heavenly Father and I are Twins.

All of my Father's hope rested in His Son. The Hope of Heaven was an infant.

Father could not heal His children without a Savior – without His Son. He and I, and every person who hoped healing for a loved child, needed Christ for hope to be realized – and real. The hoped-for Hope of heaven and earth was, and is, the Son.

This Hope began before the world was formed, when the Son said to the Father, *Here am I. Send me.*

Imagine our Father's heart when the Son entered this world in Bethlehem. He must have thought, *So it begins. The confirmation of all promises begins.* I then think of an exhausted and mortal God who declared *It is finished.* In simultaneous thought, the Father's weeping and grateful heart said *It is finished.*

I believe I echoed the same grateful utterance with my crying heart as I witnessed from heaven that Hope was not faith any longer, but concretely real.

How can I possibly express how I honor my Father for the honor He gives His Son? In Godly completion and perfection Father describes our Savior, the Hope of heaven and earth, as **My Beloved Son.** Yes, He is Beloved. I bless His Name. Because of Him I may have hope for my wounded children. That hope is more precious to me than the hope He gives me for myself. Because of Him I have hope to offer those I love.

I had only one gift to offer that Christmas, or any day of any year. So I offer to you the same offering my Father gave me that year, the offering I saw anew – an infant and Beloved Son.

Joyful Christmas Hope to you – and those for whom you steadfastly hope.

Capacity to Live

IN 2002 I FOUND MYSELF unemployed and looking for a place to live until I could get back on my feet. It took eleven months before that blessing came my way.

During that time I became increasingly depressed, despondent, and fearful. As I was entirely dependent on others for food, shelter, transportation, and medicine, I felt I was only a drain on resources and had nothing to give. I could see no purpose to my life.

I desperately wanted my life to be over.

I felt myself dying a little more each day. Breathing was difficult. With all my heart I wanted to go to sleep and never wake up.

To add to my despair I found I could not speak of my feelings without being in trouble. I was scolded and told to repent. This only increased my desperation as I saw my wickedness while I was praying for help in finding employment. I was told that if I did not repent of my feelings God would never give me a job.

I felt entirely alone and without hope. How could I hope for help from heaven when I was so patently undeserving of it?

Suicide was constantly on my mind. In my desperation I went to a friend for a blessing. I feared what I would hear – my Father's disgust and hot displeasure – but in the irony of life, I knew I had no place else to turn. So I turned to the priesthood, someone who was a safe place for me to go, and my Father (in fear and trepidation).

I am so glad I did. Rather than scolding I was given understanding and compassionate love. And a blessing. A short blessing. I don't remember anything else that was said. Just this,

I bless you with the capacity to live.

After the blessing, I went back to the place I was staying. I went to bed. I thought, *I'm still alive.* In the morning I woke up and thought, *I am not dead.*

I was numb. I did not want to live, but I was not actively thinking of my need to be dead any longer. Each night and each morning was a dispassionate awareness that I was not dead – I was still here.

I knew it was because of the blessing. I was not glad about it; I was not sad about it. There was just a resigned awareness – *I am still alive; the blessing is working.*

After a few weeks I found a job and an apartment where I could walk to work (I had no car). Things began to get better.

I think about this time of my life and shudder. It was a very close call for me. I felt cut off from the rest of the world, entirely unworthy, and cast out. On the occasions when I tried to share my feelings I was immediately sorry and felt I had further proved how alien I was in this world.

And then came my Father, my Savior, and the Holy Ghost. It is a marvel to me that the Holy Ghost was able to talk me into seeking a blessing, and that I listened and turned to the one person who may have said the words that I needed to hear.

So here I am. Still. Because my Father and my Savior gave me the one thing They have always given. Perhaps it is the only thing They ever give.

Capacity to Live.

A Football Testimony

I AM A HUGE OREGON Ducks football fan. This last weekend they played Stanford and the game was on ABC - which meant I could watch it! Hooray!

So I settled down to watch. Oregon had turnovers. And it seemed like every time Stanford got the ball, they scored. By half-time the score was Stanford 21, Ducks 3.

I wasn't sure if I had the courage to watch the second half. But I did. All I know is that the team that came back on the field for the second half didn't seem like the team that left the field after the first half.

Final score: Stanford 31, Oregon Ducks 52!

I was so excited for the last quarter I didn't have any language left - I just screamed.

You know what the Ducks did at half-time? They gathered together in the locker room and listened to the coach. I don't know what he told them, but it was good and they listened and it worked. He knew his players and what they needed to hear.

GREAT GAME! Soooooooooooo glad I watched the second half.

Well, I told you that so I could tell you this. Sometimes in our lives we may feel like we're losing the first half of the game. We may want to walk off the field. It may seem like a waste of effort - the opposition is just too strong.

So, here's what I'm saying. When you feel like your game is not going well, you need half-time. (Or call a timeout.) Because you need to talk to the Coach. Let Him call the next play. Quit trying to win the game all by yourself. Remember, your Coach knows you, He knows what you need to hear - and He knows what you need to do to win.

Don't quit at half-time. Meet with your Coach. When you walk back out on the field . . . you won't be the same person who walked off.

Your fans will be cheering.

The Great Rescue

THIS WEEK I WAS ABLE to watch parts of an extraordinary event. Thirty-three miners had been trapped approximately 2300 feet underground for 69 days. Seventeen of those days the miners were out of contact with those attempting to rescue them - the rescuers did not know if there was anyone left alive to rescue. The humidity and heat caused great discomfort and health problems - as did the need for oxygen, water, and food.

When the rescue shaft was completed it was a 28-inch diameter shaft with a narrow rescue capsule that brought up one man at a time. Six rescue personnel descended - one at a time - to prepare the miners for their ascent. All thirty-three miners were brought up and the rescuers were brought up after all the miners had surfaced.

Each day the miners had religious service and when a bore-hole was made that could send supplies they asked for Bibles and religious material. After being rescued, Mr. Sepulveda, one of the rescued miners, said, "I was with God, and I was with the devil. They fought, and God won."[2]

I watched the rescue and wept with the rest of the world. We wept with relief and gratitude and recognition that after all the rescuers (hundreds of people were involved in this effort from many nations) and the miners could do, after all their careful and meticulous preparations for safe restoration of the trapped miners to their families, it was a miracle that it worked. God made up the difference.

I think of the song *Out Of The Deep* in John Rutter's *Requiem* (see Psalm 130). How often have I cried unto my Lord - out of my deep!

And so I remember that other Great Rescue - surpassing any other attempt to save any man, woman, or child from peril of any kind.

My Rescuer is my Bread of Life and Living Water. He is my Light in the darkness of my soul. The path of rescue is strait indeed, and narrow, and He comes to me and shows me how to make the journey. He is the Way.

After all I can do - my Lord and Savior makes up the difference.

My Lord and my God fought Lucifer for me - and He won.

Still weeping with gratitude.

For Unto Us A Child Is Born . . .

WE ARE CONTINUALLY TAUGHT THAT the Atonement is Infinite and Eternal - eternally in effect; infinitely applicable . . . all-encompassing.

The breadth and depth of the Atonement are astonishing. Before I was spiritually begotten of my Father in Heaven, the Atonement was there to bless me and lend its hope to my very existence - else Father could have had no purpose in having children. The Atonement is *His* Hope, too.

I began to partake of the Atonement at my spiritual birth. Simultaneous with my birth I partook of the indescribable gift of agency, whereby I might fulfill the purpose of my creation.

I partook again when Christ created this Earth.

I received the Atonement when I gained my mortal body and was given the Light of Christ.

The effects of the Atonement were again present when I was baptized, received the gift of the Holy Ghost and the name of Christ.

I partook of the Atonement when I entered the Temple of God, received my endowments and sealing blessings: all the Mercy and Hope of the Atonement opened again to me.

The Atonement weekly blesses my life as I partake of it through the Sacramental ordinance.

Moment by moment I receive the Atonement as I repent and am healed from my sins.

Moment by moment I receive the Atonement as I am healed of the wounds of the sins of others.

I begin more fully to receive the Atonement as I am merciful and forgive others, aligning myself with its Saving Love, Mercy, and Hope.

And more completely do I partake of the Atonement when increasing gratitude opens my heart and eyes to see, comprehend, and embrace the small and significant details of the Atonement's Saving Love. I am newly aware of colors, trees, grass, rain, flowers, music, physics, family, fireflies, the ability to see, hear, feel, speak, walk, think, learn, and love. I bless my Father's heart for the details of His attention in blessing His children. By the Atonement is the creation of all things.

Because of the Atonement, my own truth and light are enlarged, increasing my sensitivity to its minute details and my capacity to embrace them.

In all things the Atonement is Infinite - there is no blessing outside of it; there is no good thing not embraced by it.

In all places and times it is Eternal. There is no where or when outside of its sphere.

The Atonement is a gift older than time and newly given every moment.

Jesus Christ is *my* Atonement. He is my Everywhere. He is my Everywhen. He is my Everything.

He is *your* Atonement. He is Now. He is Here. He is *All* . . . Yours.

Receive and Adore your Christmas Gift.

Unto Us A Son Is Given!

Football, Dandelions, and God

I LIKE FOOTBALL. I LOVE to watch a receiver maneuver his way through the opposing team to get where he needs to be to catch a pass. Some passes are not thrown very well and the opposing team is to his left, his right, in front, and behind him - trying to stop him. Yet the receiver makes every effort to catch that ball! He grabs the ball out of the air - sometimes while he is being tackled by the other team - then he tucks the ball in close to his chest so he doesn't drop it. The ball is his most prized possession.

So cool to watch. A good receiver can make some MAJOR moolah in professional football; it is one of the highest paid positions on the team.

For catching a ball under daunting circumstances and taking care of it.

I have six children (all grown now). At one time or another each of my children came to me with a dandelion and presented it as if it was the most beautiful, precious flower on earth.

You may be certain I received it the same way. I put the flower in water, praised them and thanked them. I loved receiving the flower and the child who gave it.

The funny thing is that a dandelion is a weed. Yet I never saw a weed when they gave me the flower - because the weed became a flower when it became their gift of love.

Well, here is one of the great things about God. He is the BEST Receiver in the Universe. There is no opposing force that can stop Him from receiving any gift we give. He always knows when we are trying to pass our ball - the love / gift we have for Him. It doesn't matter how poorly we throw or how imperfect our offerings are. They may look like weeds to someone else, but He sees only flowers.

He is always at the right place to receive us - and if it looks like He waded through all the opposition we sometimes place in our lives (our sins, follies, weaknesses, attitudes) to get to just the place at just the time we will be throwing out our love, well that is because He did.

He does.

If He makes it look like He stood at just that spot waiting to receive us, well, that is because He did.

He does.

He treats my dandelions like they are His most prized possession. He makes me feel like a flower.

You know how a football game is started with a coin toss? The winner of the toss gets to choose if they want to kick off or receive?

Our Father *always* wants to receive.

If we want to be like our Father we need to be better receivers. We need to get better at wading through the opposition - no matter how daunting it is. We need to patiently watch until the ball arrives. We need to criticize less about how the ball is thrown, and be more grateful it was sent.

We need to get better at recognizing the flowers instead of looking for weeds.

We need to *want* to receive - because ultimately this was never about giving dandelions, seeing flowers, or not throwing straight. It's always been about Hearts.

Betrayest Thou With A Kiss?

WHEN JUDAS LED THE MULTITUDE to Jesus, he told them that the man they sought to capture, accuse, and murder, would be the man he approached and kissed. Judas could greet the Savior in this way because he was one of the Savior's chosen apostles, a disciple, a friend. This token of affection between them would be appropriate - as a gesture of respect, loyal affection, mutual trust.

I think Judas knew the Savior well and knew this essential truth about his Lord: Jesus Christ was a safe place for him. Jesus loved Judas.

How awful for the Savior to be betrayed by such a token - a kiss given outside the context of love. The act became a lie and a betrayal.

A hard principle to correctly teach is the law of chastity. It concerns powerful feelings - and feelings of power. We are vulnerable to that power, it is tied to emotional and spiritual health - even physical health. The consequences of its misuse affects not only the persons involved, but the lives of others for generations to come.

It is an act of extreme vulnerability, an act of generosity, unity, even healing, comfort, and truth. It is an act of love.

It can be twisted into an act of selfish dominion, abuse, wounding, confusion, fear, power for the sake of power. It can be made a lie to tell a lie - an act of betrayal.

It can be easy to be fooled and not know the difference until much later, when hearts and lives are broken.

Our Father knows this. He has blessed us with a guide that will help us be free to celebrate all the joy and pleasure of the marvelous gift of sexual expression - and that is the law of chastity. The purpose of its existence is to prepare and protect His children. In simplest terms, the law of chastity tells us that sexual relationships may occur only in the context the Lord has set: marriage between a man and a woman.

Outside of that context we are not prepared to receive the joy of that expression fully, nor are we protected from the misuse and confusion that comes when we indulge ourselves out of the proper context.

The power of the feelings is so great, our culture is so inundated with enticements to lure us into breaking this law - including the false attitude that there is no real law to break - that it is incredibly easy, for a wide variety of reasons, for us to fall victim to temptation and find ourselves guilty of sin.

Out of context sexual relations become a betrayal in a relationship that has not been prepared for such intimate and vulnerable behavior, a relationship not protected by a marriage covenant - man's or God's. We become confused about our own worth, the worth of others, and the meaning of the act itself. When we break the law it is a serious sin.

The law of chastity is tied to Godhood, procreation, unity, love, intimacy, and the value of a single soul. The greatness of the sin is tied to the infinite worth of the sinner - the sinner betrays self when this law is broken. Yet some have tried to preach the seriousness of the sin by comparing the sinner to a chewed piece of gum that no one would want - making it sound as though the value is gone. The sinner is hopelessly condemned.

Well, I can't find that anywhere in the scriptures. I do find that the Savior told the adulterous woman, *Neither do I condemn thee: go, and sin no more.*[3]

This is not so easily done - having fallen once it is much easier to fall again. The Savior knows this. He does not ask us to do the impossible - rather, He makes careful provision that repentance and return to virtue is possible. He prepared the way for us to *go, and sin no more.*

It is called the Atonement.

The sinner has not lost value in the sight of God. Rather, the Atonement is an affirmation that sinners are still greatly valued by God, and are eternally invited to come to Him and be healed of our sins. Because of the Atonement we have access to an amazing promise, Isaiah says *though your sins be as scarlet they shall be white as snow; though they be red like crimson, they shall be as wool.*[4]

We need to understand that in the process of repentance we change. We are no longer the person who committed the sin. That old person dies. The new person is, then, sinless.

Clean. Virtuous. White. Pure.

That is why sinners (and we are all sinners) are not condemned. That is why there is so much Hope! Virtue really *is* its own reward - our virtuous desires and behavior bring us to . . . restored virtue.

This is the kind of Father and Savior you have. This is how carefully They give you the gift of marital relations (a marvelous gift) and a law that governs the use of the gift and protection from the anguish of its misuse. And, with compassion and understanding, They prepare a healing way of restoration for us when we fall.

Not easy, but it *is* possible.

I say again: the plan of our loving and merciful Father is in effect. Hope, repentance, forgiveness, virtue restored . . . Godhood ultimately attained.

Glorified And Glorified Again

A FRIEND OF MINE, I will call her Susan, recently shared with me that she had been molested when she was a young child. This was told with concern and not a little trepidation. No matter how well you think someone loves you, there are things that are fearful to disclose. You can not be certain of another's reaction - but she trusted me enough to take the risk.

A true blessing to me, to be so trusted with this tender and painful experience!

I have long felt that if we desire to be like the Savior we must gird our loins - for He is a God of experiences, that He may know how to succor His people. Thus, to be like Him requires experiences - not one experience, but many. Because if our heart becomes like His heart, if we choose to love as He does, and not be found wanting by lack of experience - then we will lead a Godly life, with experiences!

I found myself praying to be a good friend while in the temple a few days later. I was sitting in the chapel and reached for the Bible. I thought to turn to the Gospel of John, one of my favorite people in the Universe. How well he writes to the heart of things!

I came upon John 12:26-28. I read it once and then again. When I came into the Celestial room I looked for a Bible and read it again. I had read this before - but the meaning was entirely new.

It's this.

We are at times asked to drink from our own bitter cups - and, as in verse 27, our soul may be troubled, and what shall we say? *Father, save me from this hour!*

And yet . . . and yet. If we had no veil drawn across our memory and knew the wholeness of our lives as we were told it before we came here - we may say that *for this cause came we unto this same hour* from which we ask Father to save us. Even as our Redeemer knew His purposeful hour had come.

In great reverence and unspeakable humility, the Savior speaks further, *Father, glorify thy name.*

And Heaven answers, saying, *I have both glorified it, and will glorify it again.*

How is Father's name glorified? Jesus Christ embodies in symbol and actuality the Glory of the Name of God.

Father had already been glorified in Truth and Light when the Son offered Himself as Savior, Only Begotten Son in the flesh, Advocate, Redeemer - the Atoning Sacrifice for all . . . before the world was made.

Father was to be glorified again in Gethsemane, on Calvary, and in the garden tomb.

Now go back to verse 26. If we serve Christ we will follow Him through life, we will be where He was, having experiences that cause us to exert all effort to follow His Godly example as we endure them. We will be where He was - wounded, hurt, betrayed, suffering, broken-hearted, calling upon our Father with troubled souls to be saved from our own hour of anguish.

And . . .

We will be where He is now - using our own experience to succor others in *their* experience - because is not that the purpose to which a God uses experience? That no one may be as alone as the Son of God on Calvary - is *that* not why He accepted that lonely hour, drank that bitterest cup - that *we* would not be alone?

So that Susan is not alone, shall I choose to receive her sorrow, her pain, her wounding with the understanding and compassion I have learned from my own experiences?

In Susan's future, shall she choose to receive the sorrow, pain, wounding of others with the understanding and compassion she learned from her own hour of troubled soul?

And at those times shall we not be like the Savior and be grateful to see the fruits of our hours of experiences, our bitter cups - because neither were *we* saved from *our* hours and cups, but rather trusted to endure them?

Isn't *this* the heart of Life? Isn't *this* why we are here? Isn't *this* the Divine Essence of our Divine Nature?

And shall not our Father say, *I am glorified again?*

Let Him Hold You

WHEN MY YOUNGEST SON WAS seven months old he had surgery to relieve a problem he had had since birth. The danger in the healing process was that the wound would heal outside first, and enclose the inside hole and terrible infection would result. In order to prevent that dreadful situation I was required to force open the rapidly closing outside skin, flush the wound with peroxide and insert a swab to keep the outer parts from closing before the depths had a chance to heal properly. I had to do this several times a day.

There was no way to prepare this infant for the procedure and no way to explain why I was doing what I was doing. It was so excruciatingly painful that his tender body arched with pain and he screamed until he made no sound. When it was over we were both drenched in sweat.

My great fear was that he would associate his agony with his mother and would cease to love me. However, each time when it was over as I reached to pick him up and comfort him as best I could, he also reached to me and snuggled in to me. He would fall asleep with exhaustion.

I was so grateful to him for loving me and receiving my love for him - still! And although he has no memory of this, I do and I feel anew the horror at what I had to do, how much I hurt him, and I can still see his agony.

What caused his great distress? He was born into an imperfect world with a mortal body. Life happened in its own way. The course of nature. There was no malice in it - it was just part of the many things that happen to God's children in this imperfect world. I could not prevent it, but I could stand by him and help him heal.

There are those who believe that God ordains all things. That He causes disasters of health, nature (they are often called acts of God), and man's inhumanity to man, My heart aches for Him when I hear these kinds of comments!

We knew before we came that this world would be fraught with difficult, painful, even fearful experiences. We wanted them. We wanted the kind of life that would allow us to develop our Godly attributes and become like our most Excellent Father! To be developed to a lesser degree by lesser experiences would not attain our goal - we want Godly lives thereby to become Godly children.

And we get them.

In whatever way you may wish to look at it - healing us from the inside out and not leaving us alone to deal with our painful and fearful circumstances - Father is the place to turn. He does not cause the disease or disaster or betrayals of life, but He is committed to be with us, to help us heal, to hold us in our pain.

And God our Savior was covered in bloody sweat so that we would be made whole.

God is NOT the author of our distress. He IS the Author of our healing - reaching to hold and comfort us - and how He hopes that we do not misunderstand Him and turn away! Reach to Him, receive Him, be enfolded in His arms (even as my son was held so tenderly in mine) and rest.

It's NOT Okay!

SUZY AND BILLY ARE PLAYING together. The next thing Mother hears is a scream from Billy. She runs into the living room, Billy is crying and Suzy is trying to disappear. Mother asks what happened and Billy points to the blocks - scattered all over the floor - and Mother finds out that Suzy kicked the tower that Billy had worked so hard to build

Mother looks at Suzy and Suzy looks down. She says, "It was an accident." Mother looks at Suzy harder, and Suzy turns to Billy and says, "Sorry."

Billy is not appeased. Mother says, "Billy, Suzy just apologized. What do you say?"

Billy, clearly still upset, says, "It's okay."

Mother tells them to *play nice* and returns to the kitchen.

This is essentially what I learned that forgiveness meant - we are supposed to say *It's okay*.

Here's my problem. I have lived long enough - 64 years and counting (but not out loud) - to know that if someone owes someone else an apology it is NOT because what they did was okay!

I endured some pretty severe abuse from my husband. I spent a month in the hospital and was not expected to live. By miraculous priesthood power, and a top-notch surgeon's attentive care, I lived to raise my six children. After leaving the state where we lived and getting a divorce I discovered that I was not the only one who had suffered from my husband's evil choices.

I said prayers for my children's sake, but knew for certain I was going to hell because there was no way in the Universe I could say *It's okay.* And forgiveness is a commandment.

I spent years wishing that my children's father was dead so we could feel safe.

I was able to get supervised visits for the children's sake. He was not allowed to come to the house or near it.

Some years went by. The problem of forgiveness still plagued me. One day while I was driving home from work I suddenly heard in my mind, *Forgiveness is not trust.*

A feeling of light washed over me. A wealth of understanding flooded me. This is what I learned.

When Christ entered the Atonement He did not do it with a list of names of those who would repent, change, and receive God's forgiveness. He didn't need a list because the Atonement is for everyone. He invites all to receive it.

Of all the things that make up the difference between Christ and Lucifer - the Atonement is the defining difference. Lucifer's plan says that if you sin you are done. No hope. No repentance. No forgiveness. He had no desire to provide a Savior!

Christ embraced our Father's plan and offered Himself as Savior. The Atonement is God's witness that there is more to us than our sins. We can use the power of choice to be like God. And if we choose wrongly - there is still choice! Because of the Atonement, we can make another choice and repent, change, be forgiven. And go forward. We are not condemned in our sins unless we choose condemnation.

Christ and our Father want *everyone* to receive this forgiveness and go forward in their progression.

I realized an amazing thing. If my children's father repented . . . the man that did these ugly things would be dead! A new man would take his place. A good man. A *safe* man. Even a man who would spend the rest of his life trying to heal the wounds he had created. The most effective death I would wish upon him would be resurrection to a new life - death and a new life in the Atonement. Forgiveness!

Could I want that for him? Yes! I could. And I did.

Did I take away the consequences and safety measures that I had put in place?

No! I did not.

I saw that the mercy of the Atonement is available to all. I also saw from reading the scriptures that sometimes God must implement severe consequences when people harden their hearts and ripen in iniquity. His justice is often needed to bring them to make necessary changes in their lives. Justice may be necessary to bring us to the Atonement's mercy.

Consequences and safety measures can be a necessary part of a person's path to repentance. Forgiveness is NOT the same as trust!

God does not want us to make a list. God wants us to desire that *all* men could partake of the Atonement and be forgiven - even the most egregious offenders - if only they will repent. Only God knows when one of His children has reached a point past redemption!

We can not possibly know what changes may occur in 20 or 50 or 100 years. Evil hearts may come to that godly sorrow that works repentance[5] - and die, to be reborn to healing works and progression. Their sorrow when they realize the magnitude of their sins will be great - but it will bless *everyone* if they endure it.

To condemn means that we hold out no hope for change - Lucifer's plan.

I felt embraced in my Father's great love for me, His respect for what I and my family had endured and must still endure. And I felt His certain wrath at what had befallen us!

Did I want to be free, did I want my children to be free, did I want anyone that man may meet in the future to be free of his abuses? Then forgiveness was the answer. Keep the Atonement open in my heart to him, keep consequences and safety measures in place, and let Father decide when or if repentance had occurred. But keep the door open.

And above all other things, my Father let me know - without equivocation:

The abuse was *NOT* okay!

Lost In Payson . . . Again!

I AM FAMOUS IN MY family for getting lost. Hang two blankets on a clothesline, put me between them, and I won't find my way out. Really.

A few months ago I went to Payson to attend a missionary homecoming talk. Because my car randomly and spontaneously stops whenever it wants to, I can't drive the freeway. I had to take a back way. I had never been to this chapel before, but I thought I could find it. I prayed before I left, and I gave myself PLENTY of time to get lost and found again and still not be late, and - to my surprise and awe - I went right to it. The meeting was wonderful and I left. I had a generous two hours before my 3:00 Young Women's meeting at the hospital in Provo and figured I would have no problem because all I had to do was backtrack my way to Springville. Once I was in Springville again I knew I could make my way to Provo and the hospital.

By the way - let me just tell you that on my way to the homecoming I thought I should stop and fill up with gas. I debated myself, because it was Sunday, but I thought I should do it. So I went to a gas station. It wouldn't accept my card no matter how many times I put it in. Getting annoyed, I went to the door of the attendant's station and saw that it was closed on Sunday.

So I almost went on my way without getting gas - but the feeling kept nagging me and I went to the other end of town and got gas there instead. So . . . I had a full tank of gas. Which becomes significant later on.

Well, I left the chapel in Payson and went to the same light and turned on the same road I came in on. So far, so good.

That was the end of the *so good*.

I drove and drove and drove. There was a thunder-and-lightning storm, some hail, and huge raindrops and I passed a cemetery that I didn't remember seeing on my way *in* to Payson. But I figured that was because it was on the opposite side of the road when driving to Payson and I just hadn't noticed.

I drove quite a while without seeing other cars or any buildings.

Then I came to several buildings and suddenly I was in a town. I didn't know which town. There hadn't been a sign. But! Good News! I saw a *One Man Band!* I have a son who has worked at all the One Man Band's in Utah County! So I called him and told him I was in the parking lot of a One Man Band, but I didn't know which one and I was lost. I could hear him roll his eyes. He asked what town I was in (I know, that seems pretty basic, but sometimes it isn't . . .). I told him I didn't know. So he had me describe the street in front of the parking lot and I told him how it curved and he told me . . .

I WAS IN PAYSON!

I think I yelled at him. I told him I had been driving for AGES and I couldn't be in Payson because I had been leaving it!

Then I said I would try again and he told me to call if I was lost and he would come get me and let me follow him home. I didn't try to explain that if I was LOST I wouldn't be able to tell him where I was because if I knew where I was I wouldn't be lost. It wasn't that I didn't know where to *go* from where I was - where I *was* was lost from where I knew how to *start* going anywhere.

So I pulled out of the parking lot and made a turn and started driving. Trying to leave Payson. The second time.

I kept driving. Eventually I saw a sign that said Salem, which I had never seen before. Then I drove past a sign that very kindly welcomed me to Santaquin. I didn't even know where Santaquin was (obviously - I was *in*

Santaquin and still didn't know where *I* was). I wasn't even sure I was still in Utah County.

So I turned around and got back on the road I drove to get *in* to Santaquin (though not purposely) and drove out of it.

And drove. And drove.

I wound up back in a town. I did not know which town. Again.

I saw a Walgreen's and pulled into the parking lot. A young man was getting in his car. I stopped him and asked him where I was.

I was in *PAYSON!*

I told him I couldn't be in Payson because I had been *leaving* Payson for HOURS! He looked at me strangely and I knew then that I sounded quite demented. I asked him if he could tell me how to leave Payson. Please.

He said he wasn't very good at giving directions, but the Walgreen's manager had lived there all his life and was good at giving directions. He told me his name. I went inside and asked for Bill. He came; I explained my problem. He gave me directions. Very SIMPLE ones. And they took me right to Springville and from there I got to the hospital in Provo. Five minutes left of the Young Women's class.

We had a good laugh.

My family loves this story because they think it is solid evidence that they have not rolled their eyes at me in vain all these years. They have rolled their eyes so hard they think they deserve medals for still being able to walk upright.

I do not drive anywhere *near* Payson now. It is my personal black hole and I don't know where its event horizon is - and I don't want to find out!

Well, I told you that so I could tell you this.

Sometimes we get stuck in Payson. Our personal black holes suck us in and no matter how hard we try to leave, we wind up back in the same place.

We can spend HOURS (months, years) trying to leave. Trying to figure it out on our own. Winding up in places we don't recognize only to find out . . . we are in PAYSON . . . AGAIN!

Quit trying to do it on your own. Get directions. From Someone who has been there and knows all the roads. And can give you clear guidance.

Then follow the instructions. I almost doubted Bill's directions. It couldn't be that simple - just go to the street in front of Walgreen's and turn left? Stay on that road and don't get off? How could it be that simple? But I realized that he couldn't possibly get me more lost than I had been all day - so I decided to trust him. Good thing!

Jesus Christ knows the way out of your Payson. Any Payson. All Paysons. His instructions will be simple and direct. He knows how to get you back home!

You just have to stay on the road He leads you to, don't turn left or right - just keep going. It will take you directly Home.

And here's another thing.

Sometimes our Savior knows us well enough to see where we are headed. He may fill our tanks (as much as we will allow) so we won't run out of gas before we get help.

(By the way - we are never so lost that He doesn't know where we are, how to get to us, and how to get us Home. Even when we are in Payson.)

Get A Drink!

I HAVE A HARD TIME *remembering* to drink water. I get so focused on what I am doing that I don't pay attention to my thirst. So, I don't know I'm thirsty and . . . I forget to drink. .

I am so good at blocking out everything but work - I forget to take care of myself.

Too bad I can't take one really good drink of water and have it last the rest of my life. But I can't - my body continually requires water to keep it refreshed, cleansed, healthy, renewed, and able to function well.

I need my own personal drinking fountain by my side - just turn my head, bend down, and drink.

My Spirit and my Body are Twins. My Body needs water, chemically referenced as H_2O. My Spirit requires Living Water, eternally referenced as my Savior, Jesus Christ. H_2O keeps my body renewed; my Savior refreshes my whole Soul.

Sometimes I am so focused on my life that I don't realize I how thirsty I am. I block it out. I forget to take care of myself.

I need Living Water *constantly*: more than once a day, more than twice a day. I need my Savior *all the time*. His Living Water keeps my Soul refreshed, cleansed, healthy, renewed, and able to function well.

I am SO thankful for the Holy Ghost. He reminds me to *Get A Drink!*

I am SO thankful for the Sacrament each week. I am reminded to Remember.

It's a good thing I have my own personal well of Living Water at my side. All I need to do is turn my heart, bow my head, and drink.

Story Problems

My daughter was helping her son, Duncan, with his math homework. They came to a story problem involving a boy named Duncan. Duncan in the problem was going to watch a television show that lasted an hour. He timed the commercials and they lasted seventeen minutes. The task was to show the ratio between the length of the commercials and the length of the show.

Duncan (her son) just looked at his mother and said, "But I don't *care!*"

I don't blame him. I don't like story problems, either. I do like math; I do like solving problems that are like a puzzle. But I don't like problems that make me wonder what the problem really is.

I have been thinking about that and I decided that I am in deep kimchee. Life is *all about* story problems. For instance, doctors have a story problem every time they have to make a diagnosis in order to treat a sick patient.

Thirty years ago I was rushed to the hospital. I was in severe pain, which increased moment by moment. By the time I got there I thought I knew what the problem was; I had a broken collar bone. It hurt so bad I could barely breathe. I just wanted the doctor to fix my collar bone and send me home.

Well, it turned out that I was bleeding internally and the pain in my collar bone was caused by the amount of blood pushing against my diaphragm and pressing a nerve against my collar bone. I nearly died from the loss of blood. Thank goodness the doctor was better at *that* story problem than I was!

Often when I go to the Master Mathematician - the Great Physician - for help with my story problems, the problem that is solved isn't what I thought it was. The words I hear aren't the ones I thought I needed to hear The reassurance, however, goes right to the core of the necessary healing.

He knows the answers, He knows the medicine I need. Sometimes healing will take time (I was in the hospital a month before I was well enough to go home).

We, however, are in a rush to solve. We just want the pain to stop. But we can't solve, name, or treat, until we know the true source of the pain (internal bleeding?).

Here's the thing. If we really want to be like Him we had better get used to story problems. We need to be patient. We need the experiences that let us recognize the difference between internal injury and a broken bone. We need to be attentive, alert, and understanding. Because we need to know how to work these problems, perfectly and accurately, in all their varieties.

So to Duncan (and all the rest of us) - the answer to the *real* problem you had to solve when you were doing your math homework?

You have to *care*.

He Paid It Forward

About ten years ago a movie came out that had everyone talking about it. A little boy thought maybe he could make a profound difference in the world if he did something for someone and, rather than pay him *back*, they paid the favor *forward* by helping three other people.

There is some turmoil in my family right now. Pretty serious stuff. Sometimes I find myself unable to get any air. I just feel like I can't breathe. After a bit I am okay again . . . until the next time, when the awareness hits me full bore and I find myself unable to get any air . . .

It is hard to be a parent . . . suck-the-air-out-of-your-body hard. Sometimes children get themselves into messes that take them places we can't follow. Our *love* follows them no matter where they are, but our *self* is not allowed to go with the love, to hold or hug or be *with* them.

I think about Faith, Hope, and Charity. I think about the Atonement. It is the ultimate Godly expression of Faith and Hope for His children - born of His Charitable Love.

Surely parental love seeks assurance that there *is* faith and hope.

Surely Parental Love gave the assurance that there *would be* Faith and Hope.

And surely, certainly, *resoundingly*, my faith, my hope, my charitable love can have breath, because our Savior *Paid It Forward*.

Making a profound difference in *this* mother's world.

Courage

TODAY I LISTENED TO A talk on courage. The young man who spoke said that *life* requires courage. He gave some humorous - and some profoundly moving - examples of courage. He did a GREAT job.

I think of the silent acts of courage done every day, by countless millions on this Earth. It takes courage to marry and have hope for the future. It takes courage to have children in this world. It takes courage to serve the Lord - formally on a mission or informally as a neighbor. Life is full of changes - change itself requires courage.

It also takes courage to pray for a child who has wandered so far away from light and truth that his true self can only be dimly seen. I have said that kind of prayer countless times. How do I say it? I ask Father that whatever experience or circumstances my child needs in order to change his direction and be whole again - I pray for those things to occur. And then I pray for courage.

I know I will need it.

The Atonement stands as the two greatest acts of courage in Eternity.

Jesus Christ evidenced His great courage when He stepped forth and offered Himself as Savior - before this world was created. His courage gave assurance that the *pending* Sacrifice would be *reality* now. It was precursor to the profoundly courageous Act itself, in Gethsemane and on Golgotha.

The second, and *equally* greatest, act of courage in the Atonement?

Performed by God the Father, accepting His Son's willing offer, and observing the Act itself.

Which two acts provide the foundation for courageous prayers of hope.

Do not ever doubt the courage of God. Father and Son performed supernal Acts of Courage for Hope for my son, for me, and for . . . you.

(Read *Trial By Existence* by Robert Frost. Then read *Intimations of Immortality* by William Wordsworth. Yes, Valor reigns *Even as on earth, in paradise*. And . . . yes, we do come *trailing clouds of glory*.)

Mother's Day 2011

THIS WEEK, ABOUT 11:00 AT night, I suddenly heard the most horrible scream of my life. I hope to never hear it again. It was a child screaming for her mother, in abject and complete terror. I went outside, but the screaming had stopped and I could see no one. Yet the note of fear and horror had been so complete that I went to the corner, then down the block. Something had been horribly wrong and I had to make sure it was over.

Then I heard the screams again and went back to my home - where I saw a little girl on the porch of the home next to ours. The door was open and she was crying and screaming for her mom. I went to her and asked where her mother was; she told me she was lost.

I asked if I could hold her hand and we would go in the house and look everywhere. I assumed the mother - or some adult - was in the house, maybe the bathroom. I opened every door.

The only people there were the girl and me.

I told the child we would go to my house (where my phone was) and I would get help to find her mommy. I called the police. Eventually, they got her mom's phone number and left a message for her. They had tracked down the father - divorced parents, he didn't have custody - and he came right over and held his girl. The mother got back about midnight.

The little girl was only three years old.

In April 1981 my husband beat me nearly to death. I was in the hospital a month and was not expected to survive. Mother's Day came while I was in the hospital. My six children (ages 9 months to 14 years) were half a state away from me. I did not get to see them. I was dying. I found out years later that some of them thought I was already dead and no one wanted to tell them.

This is 2011. My oldest son, who was seven in 1981, is in jail. I remember how I loved to hold him when he was a baby. He slept best when I held him. I remember how, when his father had quit coming home at night, my boy would go through the house in the very wee hours of the morning to see if we were all home. I remember his yelling nightmares, years after 1981 when I was divorced and living with my children a state away from their dad, as my boy re-lived the terror he had during 1981. His recurring dream was that his dad was back and beating me and this time I died. He dreamed it was his fault because he couldn't stop this 6' 4" man from killing his mother.

There are all kinds of terror in this world. Fear of abandonment is real. In many cases, it is not an unfounded fear. That is heartbreaking.

It is the worst kind of fear for a child.

I wanted to be the little girl's mother. I would never have left her. She would never have screamed that horrible scream that I still hear in the ears of my heart.

I wanted to be the mother in the home my children were taken to while I was in the hospital. If I could not make that beating not happen, then let me be the mother that takes care of my children.

My son has done some horrible things. I don't know how to reconcile the man with the boy that is my son. So I don't try. I just love him. I can't be with him, but there is no place he can go that he is not loved by me.

I have abandonment issues. On occasion I will suddenly remember 1981 - Mother's Day *always* reminds me of that year. Life had abandoned me then. My children were gone. I was a mother with empty arms. When I am caught by those memories unawares I cannot breathe. My body hurts all over. I feel like I am dying. I have these feelings now while I type this. It is my nightmare.

I can't get to my children!

This year is especially poignant because of my son. I can't get to him. He is not listening. So I love and wait and hope. And love.

I want to Mother all the Earth . . . I can't even mother all my children.

Who takes care of abandoned *mothers*?

Enter the Great Parent. He never leaves His children. He cannot die. He does not go to the store. He does not sneak away. He does not break up families. He is a safe place and He is not geographically bound.

He can even go to jail.

So I told the little girl she was safe and things would be okay.

I couldn't even be *with* my children in 1981.

And when I am allowed contact with my son I tell him I love him and I believe he can put his life together again.

My *Father* tells me . . . *He* will take care of the little girls, the six children with a dying mother, and the son who is in jail.

And He says I am not a *lost* mother of lost children. He takes my hand and tells me we are safe.

The Great *Why*

THERE IS A MOVIE I watch when I want to be reminded of the power of *why* the Atonement exists. The story is set in Victorian England. Five friends are serving in the military; they have trained, practiced, lived, worked, and played together. Finally, the day comes when they receive orders - they are to go to the Sudan to fight an uprising.

Harry is one of the soldiers. He is loved and respected, a leader, and popular in his company. His friends all assume that he is as eager to go as they are, to prove themselves, to win battles, and all for Queen and Country. It is their duty.

Harry, however, is horrified. He joined the military for his father, fulfilling his duty to family tradition. He does not understand the necessity to fight battles that kill people who do not threaten his home, his family, his community, or his way of life. Duty to Queen and Country are not enough to cause him to take this drastic action. He resigns his commission.

He is required to leave immediately. He does not say goodbye. Willoughby is the first to learn what Harry has done and tells the others. He accuses Harry of cowardice. Castleton and Trench also feel betrayed. The three of them brand Harry a coward.

Jack cannot understand what Harry has done. But it is Harry, and Jack trusts his heart for some undefinable reason. He does not brand him coward. He has no answers for the others, but it is Harry and he will not join in their vilification of his friend, whom he still loves even though he cannot understand him.

Harry's three friends feel most betrayed because all they trained for is to protect each other in times of danger. They would have Harry's back; Harry would have theirs. Now he is letting them down. Jack responds by telling them that *He'll be there.*

The regiment leaves for Africa. Harry remains at home, outcast by those who have heard of his supposed cowardice. He reads every inch of news of the battle and his company. He searches daily for the postings of casualties, fearing to read the name of a friend.

The situation in Africa worsens and Harry leaves England and goes to the Sudan. He does not know what he may do to help his friends - but he is Harry and feels he must go. He throws himself into harm's way, discounting the cost of his comfort, his safety, his life. And through unimaginable hardship, pain, fear, and danger, he does aid each of them in various ways.

Willoughby (the first to accuse Harry of cowardice), is leader of their regiment. Harry finds out that they are to be tricked by the enemy. Harry is captive and cannot go to them, but he sends a friend, Abou, with a message to warn them of the enemy's plan. Willoughby does not know who sent Abou, he will not listen, has the messenger flogged, and refuses to send the message on to the leading commander. The enemy comes and it all occurs as the enemy plans. It is a rout. Later Willoughby learns it was Harry that sent the warning.

As Castleton stands in the battle confusion he sees Harry riding furiously to get to him - the friend he thought had betrayed him. A beautiful look of gladness covers his entire face. He dies in the attack, Harry could not save his life. But the glimpse of Harry restored his peace.

Trench is captured and placed in a prison from which the only escape is death. Harry walks openly up to the prison gates, knowing he will also be imprisoned simply because he is so obviously English. He does not want his friend to be alone - and he hopes to set his friend free. After much suffering and anguish of spirit, and with Abou's help, Harry and his friend escape and live to return to England.

Jack is blinded and falls unconscious. Harry rescues Jack away from the battle and the enemy, saving Jack's life. Jack goes home to England without knowing who saved him. It is only much later that he finds out it was Harry.

Harry was *not* there in the way Jack expected; he *was* there in the way he was most needed.

At the end of the movie Jack speaks in a memorial service for those who fought and fell in Sudan. He says that in the heat of battle, you can't fight for ideals or patriotism. You fight for your friends. He is saying that duty is not enough to carry you through the horror of battle, but *love* will.

Well, I told you that so I could tell you this.

The great War of the Eternities was fought in Gethsemane and on Calvary. Jesus Christ, alone, entered Hell and fought Satan to rescue those He loves. And yes, He did ask that the cup be removed if it was possible. And He meant, could those He loved be saved in any other way? The answer was, we could not.

So He entered our prison and set us free.

He did not do it for duty. *Duty* could never sustain or support such sacrifice.

Love will. Love does. Love did.

He gives us warnings when we are on a wrong course of action. Listen. Trust Him. Pay attention and do what is needful.

When we feel forsaken and think we are abandoned in the midst of our own battles, we must *Look*. We will see *His* face, it will be *His* name on our lips as He runs to be with us.

We may be caught in a prison of sin. We must always remember there is One who does not hesitate to enter that place. Only love can prompt such courage! Jesus Christ, if we let Him and if we heed Him, will guide us out. He will not leave us alone along the way - He will endure with us to the end of our journey.

Finally, we come to this. In our faith, love, and trust we may find ourselves still unable to understand what God is doing.

We may even wonder about what He is *not* doing.

Then . . . we must be like Jack. We must not doubt God's heart. We must believe this: *He'll be there.*

Our Savior *will* be with us - perhaps not the way we expect, but assuredly in the way we most need.

Never doubt *The Great Why* of the Atonement.

The Reason For The Season

I HAVE A LITTLE PILLOW my daughter made for me and on it is cross-stitched a manger with a baby and the words *The Reason For The Season*. I display the pillow every Christmas. I love the message and the giver of that gift.

We all know that Christ is the Reason for this Christmas season. We can enjoy the traditions of Santa Claus or St. Nicholas, but that is tradition and culture. Christ, however, is the Joy, the Purpose, the Meaning, and the Reason for Christmas. He is the Heart of Christmas.

So . . . Christ is the Reason for the Season.

This Sunday I taught the Christmas lesson in our Young Women's class. We were attended by a distinct and precious Spirit of love. I cannot take credit for it; it was a tender mercy.

I saw a common Truth in a new way.

After reading the story of the Nativity, I held up the pillow my daughter had given me. I bore my testimony and declared that Christ *IS* the Reason for the Christmas season.

Then I looked at my girls and with the confidence and power only the Truth can give I taught something I did not know until that moment. I taught:

We say the Reason for the Season is **Christ**.
Christ says - to us - the Reason for the Season is **you**.

Remember what the scriptures teach?

And he shall go forth, suffering pains and afflictions and temptations of every kind; and this that the word might be fulfilled which saith he will take upon him the pains and the sicknesses of his people.

And he will take upon him death, that he may loose the bands of death which bind his people; and he will take upon him their infirmities, that his bowels may be filled with mercy, according to the flesh, that he may know according to the flesh how to succor his people according to their infirmities.

Now the Spirit knoweth all things; nevertheless the Son of God suffereth according to the flesh that he might take upon him the sins of his people, that he might blot out their transgressions according to the power of his deliverance; and now behold, this is the testimony which is in me.[6]

It was all about us.

And <u>that</u> is why it's all about Him.

The reason there *is* a Season is you.

Why Lonely?

ONE EASTER SUNDAY IN YOUNG Women I asked my girls to ask any *Why* question they wanted.

It was great. Their questions were pertinent and relevant. And they came with almost no hesitation at all.

Why war?

Why pain?

Why disease?

Why disasters?

The list was long. But this is the question that cut to my heart:

Why *lonely?*

We talked about the reason we are here. We talked about what it takes to practice Godhood. We talked about the purpose of life.

Then I showed them the LDS videos of the last 24 hours of the Savior's life. The class was very quiet. When the videos were done we talked about them.

We noticed that there is no music. I am so glad there is no music. We talked about the fact that the Savior had no halo or glowing light about Him. He was not a dramatic character. There were no crescendos either in the Garden or on Calvary. He seemed like an ordinary person.

Then we talked about how His life was just like ours. Our dramatic moments (and we have them) are not presaged by music that lets us know something is going to happen. Our heroic moments (and we have those, too) are not accompanied by majestic chorus. Neither are our triumphs or our failures. In fact we can walk down the street and not be noticed even as we are in the greatest pain of our lives.

Then we talked about that great question *Why Lonely?*

Did we see any *lonely* in the events of the Savior's life?

Yes. We saw lonely:

At the Last Supper when He knew it was the last meal - - and was alone with that understanding;

After the meal, when Christ told Peter he would deny knowing Him - those words were probably incomprehensible to all who heard them;

In the Garden, when His friends slept while He suffered;

In the Garden when His prayer was answered - this cup He must drink - and He felt the weight of it all descend upon Him;

In the Garden, when a lone angel of God came to comfort and support his God and knew he could not heal or stop this wounding;

After the Garden, when Christ was greeted by a kiss of betrayal from one who should have been His close friend;

In Judas' face when he realized that there was no turning back from his betrayal;

In Peter, when the cock crowed and he knew what he had done;

In Christ, when the cock crowed and He knew what Peter had done - and knew that Peter knew;

Throughout His trial before various judges, when He was condemned by those He served;

When Barabbas was chosen for mercy and the Son of Man was condemned; and

On the cross.

Why does lonely happen?

Lonely happens when we feel disconnected from our self, or God, or others. Lonely happens when we are not known or fear we *are* known . . . as a hopeless sinner. Lonely happens when we care for others who do not want our caring. It is not just that they do not return our love, it is that they don't want to receive our love. Lonely is not being noticed or known.

Lonely is disconnect.

We all have it sometimes. We may have it often. Being received is critically important to all of us - we are God's children and of all things He wants *us* to receive *Him*.

Why?

To alleviate lonely. So you will know He sees and receives *you*.

So. when you are lonely, remember that God is beside you. He does not sleep. He does attend.

Why?

Because He knows all about lonely. He doesn't need music to know when you are in distress. He knows how drama, grief, pain, fear, and lonely come unheralded and unaccompanied by orchestration.

He sees your quiet heroic moments, when everyone else sleeps.

The Atonement was all about healing Lonely.

Your Savior is at your back.

The Saddest Question

BEFORE THE WORLD WAS CREATED, when we still lived at home with our Heavenly Father, a Plan was presented - by our Father - whereby we could become all we were created to be. The plan required a Savior - one who would sacrifice self for our redemption from physical and spiritual death.

A Lifegiver.

There was One who stepped forward, who said "Here am I. Send me."

Before the Plan of Salvation was presented, Jesus Christ chose at every moment of His existence to be Godly, to be God. His heart was prepared, His integrity was ensured. He was perfect in love. Because of His Love we were promised Eternal Life.

The Atonement was in effect at that moment and the Plan could go forward. Create a world, send the children to mortal bodies, mortal existence, mortal experience . . . everything was now in order.

Jesus Christ came to Earth. A nexus occurred. He linked the certain surety of the Plan with actual reality of accomplishment.

Our Lifegiver.

On a boat with His friends and disciples (those who should know His heart best) He sleeps. A storm arises. A terrible tempest. His companions are afraid. He still sleeps.

Then comes the saddest question.

Carest thou not that we perish?

His entire existence focused on giving us Life, that we may not perish. **His** life was all about *our* Life. How lonely He must have felt in that moment - to be so Unknown.

They did not ask Him, *Can't you do something?* They did not doubt His power.

They asked, *Don't you love me?* They doubted His heart.

When our tempests beset us, do we underestimate the Heart of God?

Do we ask the saddest question?

Or do we remember: He is our **Lifegiver** - - precisely so that we will not perish?

The Miracle of Home

JANE IS A FRIEND OF mine at work. I don't see her every day, or even every week. She works in a different department on the third floor; I work on the first floor.

Here's the thing about Jane. Whenever I see her there is a light in her face that says, *Welcome friend!* It is always there. Her smile, her eyes, her face - she just glows with light *for me!*

I feel like I am home when I am with her. Safe. Known. At peace. Warm. Comforted. Wanted. Received. I belong there.

It feels like a miracle.

No matter when or where I am, whenever I think about Jane I see the same light, feel the same comfort, warmth, peace. I am safe again. I have a home.

Just remembering her I have the miracle in that moment. I should think about Jane all the time!

I often have the same kind of experience when I pray or even just think about my Father, my Savior, my Comforter. (There was a long while when I couldn't feel this, but after seeking to trust, know, and love Them, now I can.)

Whyever would I not remember Them? They are as close as thought.

Peace, comfort, healing, safety - - all are as close as thinking about the Holy Ghost, Jesus Christ, Heavenly Father. They receive me. They *want* me.

They make me feel I belong. They make me feel at Home.
I know how flawed I am . . . It's a ***Miracle***.

While thinking of all this a sudden question came to my mind and heart. *Where does God go when He wants to belong, wants to be home?*

The immediate answer was *Here! Come here! You belong here with me. I will be a Home for You. Please come here!*

And I realized that of all things in this life - or any other - that is what I want to be. A welcoming light to God. Home to God.

When He thinks of me, I want Him to feel my welcoming light.

I want to be *His* Miracle.

Born Again

ARE YOU BORN AGAIN? IS a common question in the Christian world. If you google the question you will get literally millions of hits.

Last Sunday at church I was preparing for the Sacrament and thinking about Christmas. And the Savior's birth. And getting a fresh start.

Some believe that the Savior's birthday is in April. And I thought about how that doesn't matter, because the important thing is that we honor Him. And I thought we could do it any day of the year. And I thought, **We should honor Him *every* day of the year.**

As I took the bread I realized that I was being born again. Renewing my covenants. Clean. New. Fresh. Like a baby. *Born Again.*

I thought about how every day is my birthday if I repent.

Every Sunday is my birthday when I take the Sacrament.

I thought about how that is only possible because of my Savior. Because He was born. Which brought me back to Christmas.

Then I thought of the Atonement. How His Death was a promised Birthday for us all.

The greatest agony in history. The most important Birthday in the Universe.

Then I thought, *Our Savior was born before the world was ever created. He was born when Father presented a plan and our Brother said Here am I. Send Me.*

And I realized that was His *first* Birthday.

And I thought it was *my* first birthday. But I was wrong.

Because my *real* first birthday was when Father created the Plan of Salvation. I bet He had it in place before He ever had kids. Because He knew we wouldn't be perfect, so He had a plan of success in place before we were ever born, spiritually or physically.

So here's the thing.

Happy Birthday to me.

Happy Birthday to you.

Happy Birthday to our Savior.

Every day. Every forever, before and after days exist.

Am I Born Again?

All the time.

Thank You, Father and Savior, for *ALL* my Birthdays.

Merry Christmas!

It's His Birthday! And yours!

The Transitive Property Of Godhood

PRESIDENT HENRY B. EYRING GAVE a talk in the October 2008 conference entitled *Our Hearts Knit As One*. Four years later I still think about it.

Sometimes abstract concepts become more clear when I can see them. A few months after President Eyring's talk I had the opportunity to give a lesson on unity. A spiritually powerful math principle came to mind. I was VERY excited!

The Transitive property of math is Godly. Here is how it works:

If a = b and b = c, then a = c.

In relationships we say it this way:

The friend of my friend is my friend.

I have to tell you, I was on a roll!

We are all so different in our personalities, gifts, skills, talents, interests. I decided to show some of those differences mathematically. I wanted to see what *1* looked like. Truly, the list would be endless, but here are a few varieties of 1..

$$3 - 2$$
$$1 \times 1$$
$$1^{52}$$

$$(2 \times 75) - 149$$
$$1 + 0$$
$$55 / 55$$
$$(0 \times 1{,}359) + 1$$
$$.75 + .25$$
$$\tfrac{1}{2} + \tfrac{1}{2}$$
$$-8 + 9$$
$$6 - 7 + 2$$
$$4^2 - 15$$
$$3.1417 - .1417 - 2$$
$$\text{cube root of } 1$$

And there is always this:

1

I could hardly contain myself! I was thinking of Christ's marvelous prayer, recorded in the Gospel of John (17:21-23), *That they may be one; as thou, Father, art in me, and I in thee, that they also may be one in us . . . . And the glory which thou gavest me I have given them: that they may be one, even as we are one: I in them, and thou in me, **that they may be made perfect in one** . . . .*

Now here is what I think. In Matthew (22:37-40) we are told to love God with all our *heart, soul, and mind.* And then love each other. You could accurately say that these two commandments are the foundation of all other laws, rules, commandments, covenants, ordinances . . .

Godliness itself.

It is what Gods do.

Our Father and Savior do this. They love each other this way. It is love given and love reciprocated. Making them One. 1.

Their *hearts* are knit as one.

And knit into Their hearts is the essence of our hope, our salvation, our success, our future.

They love us the same way They love each other.

The tricky part is for us to be the same.

Love God and be one with Him. And love each other the same as He does, with all our various idiosyncracies.

Or, really, we won't *be* one with Him. Or perfect like Him.

So here is the Transitive Property of Unity with God, or Godhood.

If

You are 1 with God and

I am 1 with God

Then

You and I are 1.

The friend of my Friend is my friend.

All for One; One for All

DECADES AGO I READ DUMAS' book (yes, the WHOLE BOOK) *The Three Musketeers.* Recently I watched one of the many movies made from that book.

I started thinking about the Savior and the Atonement.

He gave All for me. I am just one person. The Atonement is personal. Mine. Just for me.

He is just One. And He gave for All of us.

If I am one with Him, then I am One for All of us. Or I can't be one with Him.

We must All be for our God. *All for One.*

Our God is all for us. *One for All.*

It is the best kind of Godhood. The *only* kind of Godhood.

The Eternal Round of Godhood.

Bringing us to the Heart of God and The Single Point of Godhood. *All One.*

Like the Musketeers.

(I just want to add that there is no being alone in this. When this truly happens, we are never lonely. I look forward to that with great Hope. And longing.)

Gethsemane, the Holy Grail, and Miracles

Perhaps the most poignant moment in history occurred in Gethsemane when the Savior of the world prayed *Father, if thou be willing, remove this cup from me . . .*

The answer was *No.* So He drank it all.

There is a legend surrounding another cup, called the Holy Grail, that claims it is miraculous and grants eternal life. This Holy Grail is supposedly the sacred cup Christ used when He introduced the Sacrament to His apostles prior to going to the Garden, where He drank of the cup that would not be removed.

That Holy Grail was symbolic of what was to come. So if the Grail was a sacred cup, yet only a *symbol* of the real Cup, then I believe the Cup in Gethsemane is the most sacred of all.

It is the Cup in Gethsemane that brings salvation to the sinner. It brings solace to the sorrowful, healing to the wounded, peace to the fearful. It brings love to the abandoned and forgotten. A Friend to the betrayed and lonely. Direction to the lost. It is the Cup that makes the broken whole again.

It is the Cup of my life and yours. The Cup of our Gethsemanes.

He drank of our sorrows and sins, trials and terrors, frustrations and fears, anguish and agonies. Our sufferings and sacrifices. Our losses and loneliness.

He drank of our broken hearts. So deeply, so completely, did He drink of that Cup that it broke the heart of God.

The Holy Grail is not the symbolic cup of a symbolic sacrament in an upper room.

The Holy Grail is the Cup of the Savior's Sacrament in the Garden.

Yes, it is Holy. Yes, it gives Eternal Life.

Yes, it is a Cup of Miracles. It is *the miracle of the Cup that was not removed.* The miracle of accepting and enduring until *It is finished.*

The Holy Grail in the Garden is the source of the same miracle in our own lives. It is the source of the Miracle of the trial that remains, the Cup that is not removed.

The Savior helps us through, *all the way through,* because He drinks it with us.

The Holy Grail of my Savior's Cup is my life. Your life. He remains with me and with you, supporting us as only a broken-hearted God may, that we may endure our own anguish of soul. Our own broken hearts.

Our Gethsemanes.

The Miracle of the Cups that are not removed.

God, Help Me!

ONE THURSDAY IN MARCH 2013 I was at work and found myself growing increasingly weak. It became difficult to stay upright at my desk. In a vague kind of way I realized that I could not drive and called my son to come pick me up. I said I needed to finish something so could he be there in about 45 minutes? He agreed and I was able to make myself finish what I was doing.

As I stood outside waiting for him to pull up I became very anxious that I would not be able to remain upright and there was no place to sit. He drove up just in time and I gratefully got in the car. I found it difficult to sit up and put the seat back and he took me home.

When we got home I went downstairs, put on my pajamas, and laid on the couch. I was very weak. I watched a movie and thought I was doing better. Then I had to go to the bathroom, which was also downstairs, just off my bedroom. Once in the bathroom, I found I could not sit up. I rolled onto the floor and was unable to get up.

I lay on bathroom floor for quite a while. It was cold. Still unable to get up, I was finally able to maneuver myself into my bedroom so that I was on the carpet. I could not sit. It was very frightening. I felt I was going away from myself.

I live with two sons and they were both gone. My cell phone was by the couch in the tv room. I was alone.

I did the only thing I could do. I prayed.

My first prayer was very short and very frightened. *God, help me!*

My second prayer was very short and equally frightened. *God! Help me!*

A reassuring presence came into my soul. I had been far away from myself. I could feel my self gathering again, still extremely weak and frightened, still unable to move, but able to think.

I was not alone any longer.

I was able to pray more specifically. I lay there for a long time. I realized it was urgent that I get to my phone and get help so I prayed and crawled into the living room and got my phone. I was exhausted, but not wandering away from myself any more. I called my friends, and they came very quickly. My plan was that I would crawl up the stairs to the living room, rest, and then crawl out the door to my friends' car and they could take me to the emergency room.

I barely made it crawling up the seven stairs to the living room. I was getting increasingly weaker. Any attempt to try to get upright was a disaster - - I was scarcely able to crawl. I felt like I was dying, but I could not figure out why I felt that way. We knew I would never make it to the car, so my friends called an ambulance.

I was in the hospital four days. I had been bleeding internally - they said my stomach was *oozing blood*. I had four transfusions. I found out later I had lost 50% of my blood and had 25% restored. I am still very weak, but getting stronger.

Why am I telling you this?

I have thought often about my first two prayers that night. Very short. Extremely informal! And answered right away - - but NOT by making the problem go away.

I realized again that we are not here for Father and Savior to make our trials disappear. Without our experiences this life teaches us nothing. Like Gethsemane for the Savior, we all have cups from which we must drink.

The answer to my prayer was that He helped me. The first and most critical response for the moment was that I knew I was not alone. And, although I was still *very* afraid for a long time, I was also aware that I was not facing this trial by myself. I was also able to get a blessing while I was in the emergency room, yet another way that Father helped me in my fears and distress. Another way He came to me.

But here is the most amazing lesson I learned from this experience.

My prayer to God was an answer to God's prayer to me.

Yes, He prays to His children! He prays, *Come unto me all ye ends of the earth . . . .*[7] He also prays, *Come unto me, all ye that labour and are heavy laden . . . .*[8]

He knows our lives are too fraught with peril, distress, trial and tribulation, fear and isolation, for us to endure without Divine help. It was so for the Savior in the Garden. It is true for us.

Father's prayer is *Help me help you!* He needs us to turn to Him so we are able to receive the help He has to give.

So, in my distress, He was praying: *Nancy, Come to me so I may come to you! Nancy, Come to me and know I am already there!*

And, in my distress, I prayed: *God, help me!* and came to God . . . and found Him already there, already Come.

I could not know until I prayed. My prayer answered His.

The Atonement itself is the great Prayer of God. A prayer of faith in us. A prayer for us to *Come* and *Know.*

Pray. Come to God . . . and be not alone in your Garden any longer.

It's Not About the Cross

WE ALL HAVE A CROSS to bear - sometimes many at once. They seem to come in all sizes and shapes, but the thing they all have in common is that they are hard to carry.

Many times I have heard it said that if we all entered a room and laid down our cross, then told we could pick any cross we wanted - - we would each pick up our own cross again and walk away.

That story makes me uncomfortable. Most often it is told in a kind of *quit your belly-aching / stop whining / you have no right to complain* tone. People never speak of this in a compassionate way. And it never makes me feel better, or encouraged, or strengthened . . . just ashamed.

For one thing, we are not dummies. If we were actually able to put our crosses down there is no chance in the Universe we would pick them up again. We would leave cross-free!

It's not about the cross.

I was thinking about the Savior and Gethsemane and *His* cross. I thought about how, in Gethsemane, He prayed three times for the cup (His cross to bear) to be removed, if possible. It was not possible, so He partook. He bore the cross.

But it makes no sense to me that He chose the *cross*. I don't think He did. He chose the *love*. And here we have much in common with Him.

Before the world was created, He chose to love us and be our Savior. We needed a Savior desperately. It was a matter of life and death (both physical and spiritual) for us. He offered to be our Savior. I believe Father said, *Make certain you understand. This will be a bitter cup to drink, a heavy cross to bear.*

I believe the Savior's response was this: *It's not about the cross. It's about the love.*

It wasn't the *cross* He chose. It was *you*, and *me*, He chose. He chose the love, He chose *us*, and took the cross, drank of the cup, that came with us.

Many of us have crosses, burdens, bitter cups that we would never choose. However, before the world was created we, too, had a visit with our Father. For me at least part of the conversation went like this, *Father, let me be the mother of these children. I love them. I covenant that I will never not love them.*

Father solemnly replied, *Daughter, do you know what you ask? There will be much sorrow for you in this, there are desperate trials ahead of them and you will share in them all if you choose this. It will be very hard. The price is high.*

I believe my answer was, *Dear Father, do not speak to me of the price. It is not about the price. It is about the love.*

A room full of crosses would stay full of crosses.

The choice is never about the cross.

A room full of the people we love . . . would be empty.

We would pick up the people we love and walk away - with whatever crosses that may go with them.

The choice is always about the love.

Let God Do His Job

I had a profound experience about 20 years ago. I had asked my brother for a blessing; however, when he got to my home I had talked myself out of it. I felt Father was just going to list what was wrong with me. I was too discouraged - - and too exhausted - - to have a blessing.

Fortunately, my brother didn't agree. We went to my room and knelt. He placed his hands on my head and spoke for the Lord. When I heard the words *You have come a long way and still have a way to go*, I almost stood up and walked away. I was too tired to go any further. I had no idea of what going further looked like - - and if I did know what I should be doing next I couldn't have done it. I could not have walked across the room to be healed.

It was horrible. I had flunked healing, and God knew it.

I was afraid to listen to the rest of the blessing. I thought I would hear what others had said: *Quit living in the past. Quit feeling sorry for yourself. If you were living the gospel, you would be happy. You need to repent. Count your blessings. You should be over this by now.*

Of course, I believed it all. And it was all about what I was not doing right. If I lived right I would be healed already!

So what I heard next almost knocked me over. My brother said, *It is not your job to heal you. You don't know how*. **God will heal you. It is His job. It is not yours.**

I cannot begin to describe what that felt like. The burden of getting it right, of figuring out what I had done wrong or what I didn't do at all or what I should do next . . . all of these things were lifted away. The burden of time limits was gone (Has anyone ever told you that you should be over it, it is in the past, it was years ago, just let go and get on with life? Yeah, that is the time limit burden!)

I could live and feel and do my best just like a regular person (whatever that is) and I was not at fault. It was *God's* job to heal me! I was off the hook!

Too many of Father's wounded children feel that being healed is their burden to carry, and it isn't. Healing is what the Atonement was all about. Christ carried that burden. Only He *could*.

So. Take yourself off the hook. Let the Atonement work in its own way and its own time. You are not the Healer. You are not the Physician.

Let *God* do *His* job.

Here is *your* job: Love Him.

That is all there is. You are okay where you are. You are.

Being Here

IN MY CALLING AS YOUNG Women president in a state mental hospital branch I had many opportunities to see my testimony in a new way. The young women in the girls' unit were very restricted in what and how they could do things.

I was teaching a lesson on prayer one Sunday and asked the question, *What is the hardest thing you have ever had to do?*

One girl's answer was very short. She said, *Being here.*

I have thought about her answer often. I have had many experiences and circumstances where *Being Here* seemed nearly impossible. Sometimes I felt that life was killing me except I didn't get to die. It was very hard.

I didn't want to *Be Here.*

I have had occasion to visit a dearly loved son in jail. I think *Being Here* is a hard thing to do for him. I know that *Being Here* is hard for me when I sit in front of the glass that separates us there.

There are many situations in life when *Being Here* feels impossible.

Being Here is hard when you are unemployed.

Being Here is hard when you are chronically ill.

Being Here is hard when you are acutely ill.

Being Here is hard when you are falsely accused.

Being Here is hard when you are physically or emotionally or sexually assaulted.

Being Here is hard when you love someone who is headed in the wrong direction.

Being Here is hard when you are betrayed.

Being Here is hard when you are homeless.

Being Here is hard when you are the primary caregiver of one who used to take care of you.

Being Here is hard when you are divorced or widowed or never married.

Being Here is hard when you feel you have to do it alone.

Being Here is hard when you are in Gethsemane and the cup before you is exceedingly bitter. Our Savior prayed three times for help from his Father - essentially saying, *Oh Father, Being Here in this Atonement is VERY hard! Do I have to Be Here?*

Here is what I know. He set the example for what to do when *Being Here* in a hard place confronts us. Turn to Father. And here is what else I know. Father did not relieve our Savior from *Being Here.*

Father does not love Jesus Christ more than He loves you or me. And he sent heavenly help to succor the Savior - an angel administered to Him in the garden.

Father did not make the Savior not have to Be Here; but He did strengthen him so he could endure doing what he had to do where he was.

Essentially *Being Here* is impossible for all of us. If a God needs help to Be Here, then that is reason to believe that we need help, too. And we are Father's business - and He is ALWAYS about His business. It will still be as hard as it is - and as painful and even frightening at times. But when we follow the example of the One who KNOWS how hard it is to Be Here, when we turn to our Father so we aren't trying to Be Here alone - then it is possible.

One more thing. Don't you just know that given the choice of NOT *Being Here* across from my son in jail - I would not be somewhere else? Because far worse than *Being Here* is to know he was alone. Think of what that implies about Father and Savior. Isn't that why Jesus Christ came - and why Father sent him- so we would not be alone? Isn't that why our Savior stayed in the Atonement and finished its work? They are all about *Being Here* for us.

God bless you with the capacity for *Being Here* - and the assurance that you need never *Be Here* alone.

Walking On Water

ONE NIGHT THE SAVIOR WAS alone on a mountain praying. His disciples were on a ship at sea being tossed by the waves, for it was very windy. It was late - the fourth watch of the night - and they saw a figure coming toward them, walking on the water. They were at first afraid, then Jesus assured them that they need not fear, it was He.

Peter said, *Lord, if it be thou, bid me come unto thee on the water.*

The Savior's response was His eternal invitation: *Come.*

Peter climbed out of the ship and walked on the water to the Savior. Then I believe the wind and the waves and the sheer impossibility of what he was doing pierced his heart, he became afraid and began to sink. He cried out, *Lord, save me.*

The Savior lifted Peter up and said, *Oh thou of little faith, wherefore didst thou doubt?*

The fourth watch of the night is just before dawn, when night seems longest, darkest, exhausting, and impossible to endure. Like many of God's children, I have been awake and frightened in the fourth watch. It is then that faith is hardest to sustain.

In the fourth watch we often call out to God, *If You are really there call out to me and I will come.*

When we are assured that He is real, and really there, we may try to go to Him - but, like Peter, we find ourselves sinking.

We have an odd kind of lack of faith. We do not doubt that the Savior can walk on water.

We doubt that *we* can walk on water.

We forget that if Christ says to us *Come* that His invitation also provides and sustains the way of Coming. It is called the Atonement.

We may feel that the storm should disappear and the uncertain water we must walk upon will suddenly change to solid concrete and the peril of our situation will cease. When the water and wind remain we find ourselves trying to do something we know is impossible.

We think, *I can't do this!* and we sink.

The Savior's faith in Peter and in us is complete. He doubts not that we can Come to Him, accomplish, and endure whatever is asked of us. Our lack of faith in the Savior's faith is what makes us sink.

And even then the Savior's hand is outstretched to lift us up.

When the Savior walked on water He performed a miracle.

Because the Savior invites us to Come, provides and sustains the way, and lifts us when we sink, we also walk on the stormy waters of our lives.

That is the real *Miracle*.

Faith Precedes the Miracle

WHEN TEACHING KING LIMHI, AMMON says, *Thus God has provided a means that man, through faith, might work mighty miracles . . . .* (Mosiah 8:18)

We know Ammon is saying that if we have sufficient faith miracles will come into our lives.

We are taught that God is unchanging. The same yesterday, today, and forever. And He is a God of miracles. His ability to perform miracles is, therefore, unchanging.

The principle *Faith Precedes a Miracle* is unalterable. He is a God of Miracles. So . . . He is a God of Faith . . . in us.

The miracle of the creation of the world? *God's Faith in us.*

The miracle of His birth? *God's Faith in us.*

The miracle of Gethsemane? *God's Faith in us.*

The miracle of the empty tomb and the living Christ? *God's Faith in us.*

The miracle of forgiveness? *God's Faith in us.*

The miracle of healing wounded souls? *God's Faith in us.*

The miracle of Godly purpose and meaning in our lives? *God's Faith in us.*

The miracle of Father's Eternal love? *God's Faith in us.*

Our Father, our Savior, and the Holy Spirit - - all Gods of Faith.

Miracles are all around us.

God's faith precedes and creates them.

Our faith brings the miracle of receiving them.

The Prince of Peace

THE CHURCH I ATTEND HAS 13 Articles of Faith - they are essentially our beliefs in a nutshell. The first Article states, *We believe in God, the Eternal Father, and in His Son, Jesus Christ, and in the Holy Ghost.*

They are our goal of becoming. We want to be as They are. We believe and trust in Their integrity, Their example, and Their purpose. We trust Their means and methods.

They give us what They desire we would return to Them. They love us and prove to us we are lovable. They love us and prove to us They are worthy of our love. We trust Their hearts.

In Them we place all our Faith, our Hope, our Trust and our Love.

The thirteenth and last Article of Faith declares the purpose and intent of our lives. It says:

> *We believe in being honest, true, chaste, benevolent, virtuous, and in doing good to all men; indeed, we may say we follow the admonition of Paul – We believe all things, we hope all things, we have endured many things, and hope to be able to endure all things. If there is anything virtuous, lovely, or of good report or praiseworthy, we seek after these things.*

The first Article of Faith declares our faith in God. The last Article of Faith declares our determined and focused desire to be Godly, to emulate the attributes of the God we love.

I told you that so I could tell you this.

Luke tells us (2:14) the message of the angels to the shepherds,

Glory to God in the highest, and on earth peace, good will toward men.

John tells us in 1 John 4:10, *Herein is love, not that we loved God, but that he loved us, and sent his Son to be the propitiation for our sins.*

Jesus Christ, the embodied Glory and Love of God, came to us *Honest, true, chaste, benevolent, virtuous, doing good to all men. He believed us able to do all good things, He hoped all good things for us, and bless His broken heart <u>He did endure ALL things</u> so He would be able to succor us to endure all things in our lives.*

He sought after <u>everything</u> virtuous, lovely, of good report or praiseworthy - - in US.

Herein is love, indeed.

Such love is Peace. Such love is Good Will toward men.

Such Love is worthy of the praise of angels.

At Christmas we celebrate *Peace* and *Good Will Toward Men* . . .lying in a manger.

I wish for us all this Christmas to be true, benevolent, doing good to all men. I hope for us to endure all that is placed before us - - the disappointments, sorrows, heartaches, trials, and infirmities. My heart's desire is that we give the gift of seeking after the good in others.

I believe in God, the Eternal Father, and in His Son, Jesus Christ, and in the Holy Ghost.

I love the Prince of Peace in the Manger.

The Light That Shineth In The Darkness . . .

THESE LAST TWO WEEKS I have watched the Sochi Winter Olympics. The lighting of the Olympic flame is spectacular. It is the culmination of every Olympic opening ceremony, a moment of grand spectacle, and we embrace it. Tradition is that the Olympic torch is carried by torchbearers from Greece, birthplace and source of the Olympics, to the Olympic site of the current games. The flame is lit by that torch in the opening ceremony, to be extinguished at the end of the closing ceremony when the games of that season are completed.

The Olympic flame burns day and night the entire two weeks of the games.

I have a friend I will call Mary. I have known her for decades.

It is scarcely possible that imagination could conceive what she has endured in her life. Darkness has surrounded her and attempted to destroy her. One wonders how it did not. Certainly she has felt enveloped in it.

But she always chooses Light. Even when her doubts and fears and nightmares insist that *she* is the dark that threatens to overcome her, she has turned to the Light of Christ. Every time.

We have had many conversations over the years. Tonight we had another long talk. It is great to talk to her. Trivialities melt away and we speak only of the things that matter most - - my favorite topic. Truths come out in our conversations because we are seeking them.

I realized today when we were talking that she has always been a Light. Always. And that is why she agreed, and God permitted, that she would come to such a life of dark circumstances. Her Light did not need to be tested to be found True and Faithful. He knew already that she was a True Light, and therefore could be trusted in the darkness that would be her childhood.

The thing is that the veil was drawn between her life with Father and His assured confidence in her Truth. So here she is, without that reassurance and *with* all the doubts and fears of self that come upon her.

The healing process of decades has had much of her childhood darkness in it, but the darkness has always been other than her. She has been, and is, and will always be, a steadfast light that continues to shine.

The Apostle John said, *But he that doeth truth cometh to the light* . . .

What Truth does she do that brings her to such Light?

Mary turns her heart to God. Before this world was created and all during her mortal existence, and forever after when mortality is eons of time past - - her heart is always turned to her Father and her Savior. She loves Them. She trusts Them. Even as she may doubt herself, she does not doubt Them.

Thus she shines in the darkness of a reality that few would have the courage to accept.

I believe there are people in this world living quiet lives of Light, surrounded by a darkness that cannot comprehend, or extinguish, the Light they have or the Source of the Light they receive.

They are not being tested. They are being *trusted*.

The Sochi Olympics are all about Earth's honors.

Mary will get no gold, silver, or bronze medal on Earth for her extraordinary life.

Mary is not an Olympic athlete.

Mary is a Flame in her Olympic night.

Jesus Christ is the Torch that lights her.

Living Temples, Altars, Stones

THE DICTIONARY AT BIBLESTUDYTOOLS.COM SAYS this about altars in the scriptures:

> *A structure on which offerings are made to deity.*
> *A place of sacrifice.*
> *Altars were places where the divine and human worlds interacted.*

The Old Testament also makes references to stones in a unique way. Jacob's father, Isaac, sends Jacob on a journey to find a wife among the people of Rebekah, Jacob's mother. Jacob rests one night on this journey and has a vision in which he sees the Lord. God speaks to him and makes promises. Then we are told this (Genesis 28:16-20):

> *And Jacob awaked out of his sleep, and he said, Surely the Lord is in this place: and I knew it not.*
> *And he was afraid, and said, How dreadful is this place! this is none other but the house of God, and this is the gate of heaven.*
> *And Jacob rose up early in the morning, and took the stone that he had put for his pillows, and set it up for a pillar, and poured oil upon the top of it.*
> *And he called the name of that place Beth-el . . .*
> *And Jacob vowed a vow, saying, If God will be with me, and will keep me in this way that I go, and will give me bread to eat, and raiment to put on,*

So that I come again to my father's house in peace; then shall the Lord be my God:

And this stone, which I have set for a pillar, shall be God's house . . .

The Church of Jesus Christ of Latter-day Saints *Bible Dictionary* tells us that *Beth-el* means *House of God.*

The book of Joshua tells us of the twelve Stones of Remembrance. Joshua took the Israelites to the River Jordan, and God held back the waters on either side of a path He created for them to pass over Jordan to their Promised Land. God instructed Joshua to have the people gather twelve large stones, one for each tribe, from the middle of the river path and then carry the stones to the other side.

When they got safely to the other side the twelve Stones of Remembrance were placed in Gilgal. Then Joshua spoke these words to the Israelites (Joshua 4:21-24):

. . . When your children shall ask their fathers in time to come, saying, What mean these stones?

Then ye shall let your children know, saying, Israel came over this Jordan on dry land.

For the Lord your God dried up the water of Jordan from before you, until ye were passed over, as the Lord your God did to the Red sea, which he dried up from before us, until we were gone over:

That all the people of the earth might know the hand of the Lord, that it is mighty: that ye might fear the Lord your God forever.

The last story is very short and it is about each of us. The *Bible Dictionary* tells us that, at a place where Israel had twice been defeated by its enemies, God smote the Philistines and saved Israel from another defeat. 1 Samuel tells us that the prophet Samuel had to exhort the people to turn from their idol worship and repent. The people fasted and Samuel made a burnt offering sacrifice and pled with God for the people. God responded (1 Samuel 7:10, 12) and *the Lord thundered with a great thunder on that day upon the Philistines, and discomfitted them; and they were smitten before Israel.*

Then Samuel took a stone . . . and called the name of it Eben-ezer, saying, Hitherto hath the Lord helped us.

The Bible Dictionary says *Eben-ezer* means *Stone of Help.*

I have been blessed with some experiences that had me walking away feeling I wasn't certain I was still on Earth. I felt sacred, holy, humble, reverent, and very, very thankful. These experiences occurred in random places: at home, at work, in the temple, in a grocery store, in a parking lot. Anywhere and everywhere. As I reflected on these experiences I started thinking about the experiences of the prophets in the Old Testament.

Which led me to *Temples, Altars, and Stones.*

Altars were built in Old Testament times as a place of offering and sacrifice to God. Samuel made a burnt sacrifice on an altar when he pleaded with God for the Israelites. Altars were sometimes built to make offerings of gratitude.

Jesus Christ was a Living Altar in Gethsemane, His Broken Heart was the sacrifice given there. No greater Altar has ever been built than the Altar of the Eternal Life of the Son of God and Man; no more precious Sacrifice has ever been offered than the Broken, Love-filled Heart of God.

So we come to *Stones*. Christ is the rock and foundation upon whom we must all build our lives. In this context, the Stone does not weather, erosion has no effect. It will not break. It is eternal.

I love what Israel does with stones in the Old Testament.

Jesus Christ is the Living Stone, the Rock of our Salvation, because on His Altar the battle for our souls was won. Condemnation and eternal despair lost and Hope triumphed.

He is our Stone of Help. Forever.

On the *temples* our church has built around the world are these words: *Holiness To The Lord - The House Of The Lord*. We all know the temple is a sacred place. The stones do not make it holy, or the pictures on the wall. *It is holy because God is there.*

Jesus Christ lives! He lives in the body that was Altar and Sacrifice. He is our Stone and Rock. His glorified, Celestial body is a Living Temple of Godliness. Wherever He is, a Temple stands.

Jesus Christ is a Living Temple.

God does not have rutabagas for kids. Giraffes don't give birth to puppies. When you plant a carrot seed you will not be harvesting watermelon.

There is an order of Truth here. It runs deeper than Nature. It extends to the Heavens.

Strawberries beget strawberries.

Elephants beget elephants.

Gods beget gods.

There are many living temples walking the Earth today.

You and I are children of God, practicing godhood. *We are living Temples.*

We are mortal *and* children of God. Mortal is about our earthly bodies. Child of God is about who - and what - we are. We are sacred places.

When we battle our own weaknesses and refuse to give up, when our offering to God is a broken heart and contrite spirit, when we sacrifice all He has given us to serve Him and His dearly loved children, when we do these things, *When We Keep The First Commandment*, then within *us* is where the Divine and human interact - - to our salvation and exaltation.

We are living Altars.

I have had some holy experiences sitting on my couch, talking on the phone, at work, driving my car, in the temple: any number of places.

There would be *Stones of Remembrance* all over this world if we all did as Joshua or Jacob.

There is no place that our feet have touched that would not have a *Stone of Help*, if we did as Samuel did. And we *can* do as Samuel did. Everywhere we are we are helped, and everywhere we go we should remember being helped.

The Eben-ezer is us.

We are living Stones of Help. We are living Stones of Remembrance.

When we turn to Christ, our Lord and Savior, our Living Altar, Stone, and Temple, *we* become Sacred and Holy. We become

Temple Altar Stone

Come, Thou Fount of Every Blessing teaches perfectly that the Eben-ezer is us. Watch this to have your soul fed:

http://www.youtube.com/watch?v=nq-Q22Pf1W8

Do You Love Me?

I REMEMBER BEING SPANKED A lot when I was young. I have been spanked with a big leather belt used by my father to carry his tools when he climbed telephone poles - he was a telephone lineman. I remember that one time he broke the buckle on my bare bottom (he spanked us with our pants down, over his knee) and I bled. Sometimes he used his hand and I remember that he used a stick of kindling also (our heat was from a wood stove).

When I was about five years old, I remember that after a spanking my father had me stand before him as he held the belt and asked me, "Do you love me?"

I said, "No."

Whereupon he spanked me some more. He then asked me the same question, and I gave the same response. He spanked me again.

He asked me a third time. Knowing it was a sin to lie, but seeing no way around it, I crossed my fingers behind my back and said, "Yes."

The spankings were over.

There were a LOT of spankings in my home. And there was hitting.

When I was eleven I remember my father hitting my sister just younger than I (I was the oldest of the children). She was standing in the living room and it sent her across the room and she bounced against the wall.

My mother came in the room and started to say something to him in protest and he back-handed her to the floor.

I walked out the front door. You must understand that for a child in our home to walk out the front door without permission was a BIG no-no!

My heart was pounding. I more than half expected that he would follow and beat me. I walked around for a while. I was angry. I was furious. I was scared.

I was thinking. And what I thought was this:

There is no one in my world that will ever stand up for me. There is no one to turn to. There is no one who will speak the truth in my home. There is no one who will make me safe. If I don't do something, no one will.

I was absolutely terrified. I was eleven years old. I made a decision. I went back in the house, nearly faint with fear and determination. I expected to be killed. I didn't care anymore if I was.

My father was sitting at the table, smoking a cigarette and drinking coffee. My mother was sitting at the other end of the table. It was silent in the house. They were looking at me. I walked up to him - out of arm's length, but standing in front of him. This is what I told him:

I do not love you. I hate you. No one in this house loves you. We are afraid of you. I know you can beat me and you can kill me and you can make me say that I love you and take all this back. If I do it will be a lie because you are beating me. It will not change the truth.

If you hit my mother again I will kill you. I will get a knife and stab you to death. I will do it. I will probably go to prison, but I don't care. I will kill you.

My heart was pounding so hard I could barely speak. I expected him to leap off his chair and kill me. He did nothing. To this day I do not know why. Nothing happened at all. It was as if I was invisible or had said nothing. It was ignored.

But I felt that at least someone had spoken, someone had done something in defense of what I thought, at the age of eleven, was right and true.

I knew I was alone in this world and there was no one for me to count on but myself.

I remember the last spanking he gave me. My great-grandmother was visiting - it was VERY rare for us to have any company ever! I was in the kitchen with her and my mother. My father walked in the kitchen and told me to come into his room.

I had not been doing anything wrong, but I knew what was going to happen. We got into his room and he started to remove his belt.

I was thirteen year old. I was on my menstrual period. Faster than it takes to type this, I decided that if he took down my pants to spank me I would run into the kitchen, get a knife, and stab him to death.

Then I would run out of the house and try to escape. I had nothing, no resources of any kind, could not turn to my mother or anyone else for help, and I knew the police would find me. But that was my decision.

Fortunately he did not ask me to take down my pants. Just before he started to spank me with his belt he asked me, "Do you know why you are being spanked?"

I shook my head, "No."

And he said exactly this, "It is for all the things you did wrong and didn't get caught."

Then he spanked me.

A couple of months later my mother left him and got a divorce. This was in 1960. I was in the eighth grade.

I learned a powerful lesson from my father. I learned that parents can do anything they want to whip a kid into shape. I learned that I was inherently evil and would never be a good person no matter what I did (my badness was a function of what I *was*, not what I *did*).

I learned that parents are not a safe place.

Well, I told you that so I could tell you this.

The first of the Ten Commandments in the Old Testament really bothered me.

Thou shalt have no other gods before me. (Exodus 20:3)

The first of the Two Great Commandments REALLY bothered me:

Thou shalt love the Lord thy God with all thy heart, and with all thy soul, and with all thy mind. (Matthew 22:37)

I figured I knew first-hand what that meant. God was just like my dad.

Time passed. I found myself divorced with six children. My children had the kind of trauma you could expect from children whose mother was nearly beaten to death by their dad. Our home had the kind of problems you will find where children had been exposed to violence, fear, and sexual abuse.

As I attempted to hold my family together and find ways to help my children heal, things kept getting worse. I had moved us from the state where their father lived. I was trying to raise six children on my own and having a very rough go at it.

I needed God.

So, one evening after work I was in the kitchen trying to fix dinner for six hungry children. I was exhausted. Suddenly, I just couldn't do it any longer. Weeping, I just stood there in the kitchen and said this:

Okay, God. Faith precedes the miracle? Here's what I am going to do. I am taking my faith, like poker chips, and I am betting it all on you.

I am betting the poker chips of my faith that you are the kind of God, the kind of Heavenly Father, that you ought to be.

I can't do this alone. My children need me to function. They don't have anyone but me. I have to believe I can somehow do this. So I am betting that You are the way You should be. I am betting that You love Your kids at least as much as I love mine.

And if I am wrong, I don't want to hear about it until I am dead. Do you hear me? I don't care if I am wrong, it's hell now and hell later anyway for me, so I don't care.

Because while I am here I have to be able to take care of my kids. And I can't do that without a God that's the way He ought to be.

And I am NOT going to change my mind. So be the way You should be, because that is what I am betting on.

That was one of the scariest things I had ever done. I was close to forty years old. It was the antithesis of my declaration to my earthly dad when I was eleven.

I could hardly breathe. I expected to be struck by lightning. Really. I was sobbing. Then there was a powerful feeling in the room and in my soul. I didn't know until years later what it was.

At the same time, I also decided that I couldn't do it half way. So I decided to keep the first commandment. I started to pray, *Father, I love thee. Please bless me with the love I need.*

I didn't really know what it would feel like, to love my Heavenly Father. Nor did I completely believe that it was possible. But I had made a declaration of faith and I was going to go all the way, if I could.

About fifteen years later, I was saying that same prayer, *Father, I love Thee. Please bless me with the love I need.*

I was suddenly overcome with gratitude and awareness that this prayer had been answered years ago. I saw in my heart my Father weeping with gratitude for me for the prayer I prayed in my kitchen so many years before. I saw His tears of gratitude that I was finally giving Him a chance, an opening to my heart so He could reach me, comfort me, attend me, strengthen me, bless me, heal me, be my Friend . . . .

And . . . so He could give me the Love I needed. The thing I had prayed for, for so many years.

We have a Father in Heaven who loves us. He is the kind of Father He should be. And He is a Safe Place.

Take My Yoke Upon You

PICTURE THREE SCENARIOS IN YOUR mind. Each is a true story of my life, and perhaps of yours, as well.

In the first I am walking through my life, alone and overburdened. I have a yoke about my neck and in my mind and heart I hear the constant voice of the world:

> *You can't do this.*
> *You are alone.*
> *You aren't good enough to make this work.*
> *You are alone.*
> *You aren't smart enough to know how to do this.*
> *You are alone.*
> *You aren't strong enough to finish the journey.*
> *You are hopeless. You are doomed to fail.*
> *You will let your family down. It is inevitable.*

In reality, there are times when I have reached out to others, asking for help to believe in myself. Listening and watching carefully for any sign, word, reaction, that would let me know I was wrong about me.

Trying to find some hope. Some affirmation of possibility. Some reassurance.

Instead I have often received judgment, condemnation; I needed to repent for listening to Satan. If I prayed and repented these feelings would go away. My burden grew even heavier.

When sharing with another the heavy weight of my journey, I have been told I should not share my dirty laundry in public. My shame for my life isolated me even further; I was more alone than before.

My companion on my journey was constant criticism, endless derision, mockery, and scorn. A constant millstone.

The journey was pointless. The only thing that kept me walking the road was this: six children who had no one else to turn to.

The second scenario is very different. It is the same journey vastly changed by the Savior's invitation to us all:

Come unto me, all ye that labour and are heavy laden, and I will give you rest.

Take my yoke upon you, and learn of me; for I am meek and lowly in heart; and ye shall find rest unto your souls.

For my yoke is easy, and my burden is light.[9]

Surely I labour. Surely I am very heavily laden with burdens that seem to crush my joints.

In this part of the journey, I turn my heart to my Savior. I block out the world and the clamor that surrounds me.

I exercise faith, and pray for an increase of it.

I stand still and know that He is God.

I seek priesthood blessings, which assure me that I am loved and respected by my Father and Savior. The words are so kind. The respect is palpable. I know I am not alone. I know my burden is not dirty laundry before God, but a sacred task, a sacred grief, a sacred sorrow, a sacred affliction, a sacred repentance.

My Father and my Savior see to the very heart of it all, the center where, even though I carry it, I have not had the courage to look.

The scripture is true! I learn of Him as I see Him knowing me.

He is meek. He has no pride at all in replacing my worldly yoke with his. There is no hubris or impatience in His ready stepping to my stride. He matches me step by step, and my steps grow longer, more certain. I go farther than I ever could walking alone.

I begin to know I will not, I can not, fail.

He is lowly in heart, willing to love me as I am, where I am. I am the least of His children and he is not ashamed to be seen walking with me, in our shared yoke.

He is not ashamed.

Like the disciples in the storm in the sea, I experience the miracle of Christ telling my tempests, *Peace, be still.*[10]

There is peace.

My soul is at rest.

The third scenario is a surprise. I meet others in my journey, one at a time, at varying intervals. There is something very familiar about them. I search their faces, their situations, the droop of their shoulders, their faltering steps. Each time, I am aware it is I and not I.

Another person, heavily laden, is walking alone.

My heart aches.

Still yoked with my Savior, I walk to the others. I speak with them. I listen to them. I begin to know them. I love them. I experience a curious thing. My heart hurts like it is breaking.

I share my own experiences. I tell them I know how hard it is to do it alone; indeed, it is not possible.

I talk about my Friend and theirs, I talk about my Savior as if I know Him as well as I know myself. Because I do. We have journeyed together, He and I.

I make the invitation: Learn of Him, Turn to Him, LOVE Him, Trust Him, Walk with Him.

I tell them He is the One who makes the journey possible, even successful.

Even, at times, joyful.

I feel bigger inside, and realize my heart did break, it burst its boundary and enlarged, increased, became more Godly. My journey is still hard, but for a time I am so happy!

I look at my Savior. He is weeping. Why does He weep?

He weeps because *HE* is not now walking alone. I have become a disciple. I have become meek and lowly and enlarged of heart.

I brought peace to others as I testified of the Savior's yoke. Other burdened souls were rested for a moment, and know where to turn for more peace, more rest, more of Him.

Another surprise, all unlooked for. Down the road the friends I helped are speaking to other burdened souls. We recognize each other.

My partner and companion, my Savior, weeps again. So do I.

And so we travel. Sometimes another disciple, with Christ in his yoke, lifts me through a hard place. Sometimes I am lifting another.

We know we can only do this because it is the yoke of Jesus Christ upon our shoulders and about our necks.

More accurately:

It is the Yoke of Christ we carry in our hearts.

Father in Heaven's children on a Godly journey, together.

I marvel at myself, my God, and His Wondrous Yoke.

As God Is Our Witness, Stand As A Witness Of God

STAND AS WITNESSES OF GOD at all times and in all things, and in all places that ye may be in, even until death, ...[11]

These are words from the baptismal covenant that we make with God when we choose to take upon ourselves the Name of Christ, serve Him, and be His disciples.

They are a mirror image, a perfect reflection, of Christ's life. We study His life and read His words - - yet too often we get only half the meaning.

Yes, He stood, and still stands, as a Witness of God, our Father and His, Who sent Him to us.

Here is the other part, the best part. Because this is the part that tells us exactly what Gods do.

Jesus Christ spends His entire existence standing as a *witness of us at all times and in all things, and in all places that He is . . . even until His death . . . and beyond.*

He never forgets who we are. We are children of God. We are little gods practicing godhood.

The Atonement is all about being a witness of our Godly existence. Father and Son never forget the purpose of our creation: who and Whose we really are.

Sometimes we are not true to ourselves or each other.

The Atonement is *always* true to us, and that is why we have it.

We need to remember our covenant with God the next time we are angry or feel unkindly towards another. When another has wronged us and we want to hurt them back. Sometimes we forget who we are and damage ourselves. Sometimes we forget who *they* are and damage others.

We need to ask ourselves, *Am I being a witness of God right now? Is this what Gods do?* And then we need to be like Christ, and be a witness of the Godly child in us and in others.

As God is *our* Witness, so should we be a witness of Him and all His children.

Waiting On God . . . Waiting On You

IN 1982 MY HOME TEACHER gave me a blessing the day before I went to court and had my divorce declared final. I had six children, the youngest still in diapers. My future stretched before me like a Black Hole of existence. I was terrified.

In this blessing I was promised that I would some day be sealed in the temple to a marvelous man. On the heels of that promise I was told that before that day came I would have many hard trials.

My heart went from hope to fear in one second.

Since then I have had several blessings promising me that I would have many hard trials, and they are true. I have had those trials. But then another priesthood blessing comes along telling me there are more hard trials ahead. I have been told that if I knew what was coming I would be very afraid.

And I have had other blessings that again promise marriage to a wonderful man; one blessing called him *majestic*.

Well, it is 2014 and the hard trials part is no joke. And I know there are more to come.

As for the marriage part . . . I am still waiting on the Lord.

And I have learned some things about waiting on the Lord.

Waiting on the Lord is a sacred and wonderful and hard thing to do. It is not like waiting for a bus. You can't put life on hold until the promised blessing arrives. (You can try, but it doesn't work.)

Waiting on the Lord can be busy work. It involves reading the scriptures, prayer, church and temple attendance, fasting.

Our lives do not stand still while we wait, although sometimes it feels like they do. *Life happens* while waiting. We do dishes. We go to work. We take care of children. We get sick, children get sick, family and friends need help, there is homework, the dryer breaks, the car has a flat tire, . . . the list is endless. And relentless.

All while we are waiting for the blessing we were promised.

I have learned that waiting on the Lord for a promised blessing does not mean that other blessings cease. He is still sending many blessings every day; He has not ceased to love or bless me.

I learned that waiting on the Lord does not mean that there is no fun in my life. There are still thunder storms to revel in, there are still Star Wars movies to see (yes, I have already told my boss that I will not be at work December 18, 2015 - - I will be at the midnight showing of Star Wars Episode VII), there are still doily moons to marvel at, and there is still football season for my Oregon Ducks. Tulips still grow, and daffodils and lilies-of-the-valley. There is still the fragrance of petunias, pinks (they smell like cloves), and white flowers on trees in the spring.

I still have grandchildren who love me, children who love me, friends who love me. I still have a Father and Savior and Holy Ghost who love me.

And even more important than all this, more *critical* than all of these, I still have people to serve and bless. I still have the ability to love.

I still have the purpose of being Godly while I wait.

There are people who are waiting on *me* to deliver the blessing they were promised.

Someone else may be waiting on the Lord, because the Lord is waiting on us to answer their need, their prayer, their cry for help.

So waiting on the Lord may be that God is waiting on us.

It isn't wasted time unless we waste it.

Waiting on the Lord is a matter of faith, trust, and love. A matter of doing and being. It is not passive; it is patient. It is full of activity. It has Godly purpose.

As for God waiting on us? His wait is a matter of Faith, Trust, and Love. A matter of doing and being God. It is not passive. His wait is eternally Patient. Full of loving activity and Gentle Godly Purpose.

P.S   Look up *Wait* in the *Topical Guide* in your scriptures. Read the verses. I have marked the ones that tell me of God's promises to those who wait on the Lord. He knows it's hard. He helps us do it. These scriptures comfort, encourage, and strengthen me. Just like He promised.

Am I Hard to Love?

A FEW DAYS AGO I received a call from a long-time friend. In the past 25 years I have seen her, briefly, about three times. Almost all of our relationship has been by phone. We first met about 30 years ago and she has had some unusually rough experiences in that time. She has been extraordinarily challenged, has experienced the kinds of trials that no one wants to believe. The kind that takes ongoing, Relentless Endurance and Uncommon Faith.

And that is her life. Uncommon Faith and Relentless Endurance are the hallmarks of her daily existence.

She is an amazing woman.

She trusts me. I have loved her all this time. My ability to love her stems directly from the love I have for my Father in Heaven. He put the love in me, because I chose to love Him.

Because of my love for our Father, it is easy to love my friend. Because my heart is open to our Father's love, it is an easy choice to love what He loves, to see as He sees, to embrace what He embraces.

So, a few days ago my friend asked me a surprising question. *Am I hard to love?*

She caught me off guard. I knew the answer, the answer was easy, but the question was painful to hear. I knew she asked it because love and acceptance and respect, all those things Father had given me to feel for her, were scarce in her world of acquaintances. Even, and maybe especially, in her church family.

But I knew the answer, because I know and love the Savior and our Father.

No, dearest friend. You are not hard to love. But your life is hard for people to take. They don't want it to be true. So they don't believe it is true; they don't want to get too close to it.

And then, because I wanted her to know she was in good company, and not to be despised because of her loneliness, I talked about the Savior.

His disciples, even those closest to Him, did not want to believe Him when He told them what was coming. When the hour was at hand, His three dear friends slept through His Garden Suffering. He was betrayed - by a kiss - by one who should have been a protector. Then Peter denied Him - - three times!

It would appear that the Son of God was hard to love!

He truly understands Loneliness.

I have been thinking about this. There is something I did not say, and I will say it now.

First. Dear Friend, you are easy to love. Easy for Father to love you well enough to provide a healing Savior. Easy for your Brother to be that Savior for you, because you are easy to love.

Here is the hard part. The hard part is wading into the midst of your wounds and fears and embracing, healing, hurting, and remaining in Infinite Endurance through all of it - - ALL of it - - until you are healed.

Yet that is what your Savior did. He waded right in. He is there still. Because He knows lonely. He knows shunning. And He is not afraid of your life. He does not turn away from your life.

He embraces you and all that comes with you. Where you are, He is. Always.

Second. Second is beautiful and worth living and hoping for - - because it is Real. Second is the part that tells you what kind of Father you have. Second is what this Unchanging Father did for His Beloved Son. Second is what Father will also do for His Beloved Daughter.

He will give you 3 Nephi. He will give you multitudes of people who will come and embrace you, all of you: your heartaches, wounds, sorrows, fears, and the loneliness.

Your fierce courage. Your valiant faith.

He will give you the healing of being received - - entirely, utterly, completely. And the Savior who weeps for you now in your torments will weep with you again in your joy.

So. Yup. She is easy to love.

And so are *you*.

Prayer - It's for Kids!

THE WORST THING THAT CAN happen to a child is abandonment by his parent. Children know they cannot survive alone. Whether the abandonment is physical or an abandonment of the heart, it is devastating.

I am a child of God. I cannot survive this life alone. I can't. I need help and love and reassurance. I need my Dad.

He knows that. So, among other things, He gave me prayer.

I had been taught that there are four steps of prayer. So, one day I decided to test God and this commandment to pray. I wanted to know, *Where is the love, the personal love for me, in the commandment to pray?*

This is what I learned. And how it enlarged my soul in love and trust for my Father!

Call Him Heavenly Father or Father in Heaven. I love this part. Father wants me to remember who and Whose I am! God is my Father! I am His child! This first step lets me know I am beginning a personal conversation with a Tender Parent. He is my Dad. I am His kid.

When I pay attention to the words, *Dearest Father in Heaven*, then my heart can begin to be comforted already - gentle help is at hand!

I often picture myself very small, very young, and I just climb into His lap to talk. It is peaceful there. And safe.

I am not alone.

Thank Father for my blessings. I used to wonder why it would matter to Him if we did this second or third. What difference would it make?

I now realize that it doesn't make any difference to *Him* - it makes a difference to *me*.

In the past there were times when I prayed that I felt hesitant to speak about what was on my mind, or fearful of disclosing what was in my heart. I felt too ashamed to ask for forgiveness. I do not feel that way any longer.

When I thank my Father for my blessings, I have to think about them and be aware of them. In this way I am reminded that He has blessed me in the past. He has never failed me. When I have asked for a bitter cup to be removed - and He has not removed it - I remember that He has helped me endure the unendurable. I can see how I have weathered trials and tribulations that I thought would surely destroy me. And in the process, I became more than I ever believed I could be.

Thus, I am encouraged in my prayer. I know it is safe to ask for His help because I remember He has helped in the past.

When I share the joy and triumph of my blessings (I studied hard and prayed for help on a hard test in school and I aced it! Yay!) I realize that my Father rejoices with me in my successes - no matter how small. Just like a real Dad!

The process of remembering and being grateful to Father for His help brings peace and rest to my soul. I am humbled, strengthened, and reassured even before I ask for the help I need.

I am made aware that He is Ever-Present in my life.

Ask Father for help. My faith in my Father's love and concern for me is by this time greatly enlarged. I am engaged in the safety of His Heart and I may freely pour out my soul.

I can tell Him anything. I can tell Him Everything. I can confess my sins. He loves me. We are in this process together. We always have been. We always will be. I am aware of it.

As I reveal myself to Him, I often learn more about me than I knew before. I realize He knows me and wants me to know myself, too. I may have thought I was praying for a certain blessing and then realize that my real need is deeper and different than what I thought it was.

I think I am revealing myself to Him; He is revealing myself to me. He is also revealing Himself. It is a powerful exchange of trust and realization.

Over the years I have come to know that there is no better place to go with my intimate fears, desires, heartaches, despair, and yearnings than to my Father in prayer.

I have also learned that when I pray for others they may be revealed to me more completely.

Prayer increases my understanding of myself and others and my Father.

Even when I am talking to Him about my faults, follies, weaknesses, and sins - - prayer strengthens me in the knowledge of my Father's love and devotion and reassures me that I am not lost to Him or the Atonement. I have Hope again.

I am not alone.

Close in the Name of Jesus Christ. This is not a *See you later* or a farewell!

Remember what John said?

In this was manifest the love of God toward us, because that God sent his only begotten Son into the world, that we might live through him. (1 John 4:9)

Jesus Christ is the Name of my Salvation. It is the Name of the Tree of Life and it is the Name of the Fruit of the Tree of Life. It is the Name of my Salvation and my Hope.

Jesus Christ is the Name of the Atonement.

Jesus Christ is the Name of the Infinite and Eternal Love my Father has for me.

Jesus Christ is the Name of the Constancy and Integrity of my Father's Heart.

If I am afraid, with this Name I know I am Safe.

If I feel alone, with this Name I know I have a Friend and Father.

If I am in despair and hopeless, seeing no way out or through, with this Name I speak Hope.

If I have sinned and am filthy with sin, by this Name Forgiveness and Purity can be mine again.

If I am rejected, scorned, mocked, and denied, with this Name I am Received and Loved, Understood and Known.

When I say, *In the Name of Jesus Christ, Amen.* I am not saying *Good-bye*. It does not end the conversation. It *seals* the conversation to my heart and I can carry it with me. Everywhere. I may have climbed down from Father's lap, but we are now walking together and He is holding my hand.

The proclamation of this Name declares: I am not alone.

I *am* a child. I am Heavenly Father's child. He is my Dad.

And Prayer is for kids.

He Loves Us AFTER

I often feel that I am hard to love because anyone that loves me would NOT love me if they really knew me. So if I want to feel loved I need to not let anyone get really close because then the love, and the respect and trust, would disappear.

I often protect myself from people getting close so they won't know how awful I am and then not love, like, or respect me any more - - therefore I can't take it personal while they are loving, liking, and respecting me because I know I am not the person they think I am so it isn't about me.

So I know that when someone says they love me, or think I am, for some reason, a great person, then I know they are saying it only because of how great THEY are, because they don't really know me.

The evidence? They love me. If they really knew me they wouldn't be able to love me. It gets pretty nuts. It is either proof of my great intelligence - because Dude! This is hard to keep track of, you know?

Or it is proof of my stupidity. Because, Dude! This is crazy thinking and doesn't make sense!

And here's the kicker. How can I believe my Father and Savior love me?

Something that made a HUGE difference for me is this: One day I realized that in the Atonement, Jesus Christ saw all my sins, follies, foolishness, unkindness - - ALL my ugly places. *Nothing* in me is hidden from Him.

And I saw that the miracle of the Atonement is not that He loved me enough to volunteer to do it. The miracle of the Atonement is that He still loves me AFTER IT IS DONE!

AFTER seeing all my ugly places. AFTER! (Yes, I know, this is shouting. But AFTER? Whoa!)

So now when I pray I talk to God about all my uglies. Because now I know He knows, and knew, and loves me anyway. He is the one safe place for my uglies to go. So I talk about it. And I feel better. Because I am not carrying my ugliness alone. He helps me work on removing them. Which is what it's all about anyway.

Trust God's love for you. Believe you are lovable. Try it.

Remember. He loves you AFTER.

Where There's Life, There's Hope

NOVEMBER IS AN INTERESTING MONTH for me. My first, third, and fifth children were born in November. My first child was born on the 13th, and ever since then 13 has been my Lucky Duck number. I love the number 13. The numbers 19 and 20 also brought me Good Luck in November.

My grandmother died November 22, 1992; my father died November 24, 1998.

And on November 14, this year, my son-in-law died very unexpectedly.

A month ago, Christmas looked very different for my daughter and granddaughter than it does today. Next year looked very different. Ten, fifteen, and twenty years from now looked different. The future had a three-member family in it. But that was a month ago.

In 1981 I faced that kind of loss, although for different reasons. One minute I was a stay-at-home mom with six children.

Suddenly, I became a single mother with six children to support. We were reeling. For a VERY long time. Our future was completely different. We had to move . . . in November . . . to a different state where we knew no one except my sister and her husband. I had no car. I had no money and none coming in. I had no job. I had no place to live. All I had was fear. HUGE fear.

I was afraid of everything. I was afraid *for* my children and I was afraid *of* myself. My life and my future were out of context now. If we fear the unknown, then I feared everything. I didn't know anything. I didn't know me as a single mom and I feared I would fail my family.

I can't say it enough. I feared everything.

My prayers were consistent. In the middle of the night, because I could not sleep at all, I knelt and prayed for us all to be dead by morning. If God really loves His kids, and if we *were* His kids, then how could He say *no* to that prayer?

Here's how.

He gave us Christmas.

He gave us Infinite and Eternal Love. He gave us a Savior. He gave us the Atonement - with power to heal all wounds. Infinite and Eternal Healing Love.

Love that has the power to heal infinitely and eternally can heal everywhere and everywhen.

He can heal in this world. He can heal in the next. He can heal today and He can heal yesterday and tomorrow. He can heal forever.

He can heal our unknown futures because He knows them.

He can heal broken hearts because His was broken yet stayed whole - - and perfect - - in Love.

He can support and heal loneliness, moment by moment, because in His loneliness He stayed fixed in love and connected to us all.

He can heal sudden and abrupt out-of-context lives, because He places Himself, *in context*, in every life, all our lives.

He can heal despair because His certain Hope applies to all losses.

He can heal fear because His boundless courage transcends all fears.

He can heal deaths, of all kinds and means, because He is *Life*.

It's true, then.

In our loss of life, in all the ways we feel we have lost our lives, there is Hope.

I am writing this to *all* people - - past, present, and future. This year I am writing especially to my son-in-law - who is home with God, and his wife and daughter - who are still here. Because these words are true Every*where* and Every*when*.

So, Merry Christmas. In any *way* and any *where* that your Christmas is this year, remember this - - and if you can't be merry, then at least have

some measure of Healing Assurance and Hope - - because, even in our
Novembers,

**Where there's endless Life . . . the Savior's life . . .
there's Hope**

He Has an App for That!

APPLE HAS TRADEMARKED THE PHRASE *There's an app for that.* They use it to advertise and promote all the apps they have for their electronic devices. Anything you want or need (just about) for your personal ease and comfort in this world can supposedly be accessed in an app made for you. Download and your life is instantly better. These apps are for your convenience - - no big deal. They download through the air, as it were, and you are immediately set up with what you need.

It took hundreds of years for technology to come up with this. Electromagnetics has changed our lives.

You gotta love physics.

Before the world was created, the Great Scientist made an app for us. Using Celestial Physics, He provided an app for this Earth and all who have ever or will ever live on it. He did it before the world was created. We don't have to wait for scientific discoveries; it is already here.

It is Omnipresent. It is Everywhere and Everywhen and Everyone available.

Have you sinned and want a way out of the habits and behaviors you have embraced?

He's got an app for that.

Are you overwhelmed with guilt and self-hatred and self-loathing?

He's got an app for that.

Do the years stretch before you with no hope in sight, nothing but suffering on your horizon?

He's got an app for that.

Does life hold no meaning or purpose for you at all? Can't figure out any good reason to be here?

He's got an app for that.

Are you being eaten alive by bitter hatred and can't find a way to let go and forgive and move on?

He's got an app for that.

Do you sorrow for a loved one who is distant and lost and you fear for their future and their lives?

He's got an app for that.

Are you alone and more lonely than you ever dreamed a person could be and still live?

He's got an app for that.

Do you feel like you fail at all the things that matter - - the world and those you love would be better off without you because you just make things worse?

He's got an app for that.

Have you made so many mistakes that you think you can never be forgiven?

He's got an app for that.

Have you been promised blessings that don't seem to ever come, and you are losing hope that they ever will?

He's got an app for that.

How do you get these marvelous apps? What are they called? Who is the Software Engineer that wrote them? What language did He use - Fortran? Pascal? Cobol? Python? Java?

The Software Engineer is our Savior, Jesus Christ.

The App is the gospel of Jesus Christ.

The key component is the Atonement.

Using the Universal language of Love, He wrote it with His Life, His Light, His Compassion, His Understanding, His Forgiveness, His Healing, His Blood, His Broken Heart, His Death, and His Resurrection. He wrote it with the Love of Godly Hope and Promise.

Here is how we get it. We turn our hearts to Him. Love for Him accesses His Love for us - - and downloads His Gospel for our healing and renewal. Love for Him accesses the Atonement.

Using this App brings forgiveness and hope. It brings awareness of purpose and plan and meaning and a most valued Friend. It softens hearts and brings compassion and understanding, patience and solace. It heals wounds - - the ones we have and the ones we have given others.

We don't even have to have a Smart Phone.

We don't need satellites or electricity or batteries or interpreters.

The App is safe. It can't be hacked. It's all His. And ours.

Turn your heart to God and Love. Use His App and be loved, healed, forgiven, and able to forgive. Use His App and receive His promised Peace and Hope.

Download it today!

(This offer never expires. It is never prohibited from anyone. Age is not an issue. This App is not sold in stores. Good in all 50 states and any-where else on the planet that you may be.)

I Don't Deserve This

In April 1981 I was severely beaten by my husband. Months later I found myself a single mother with six children and no job.

Our world was torn asunder.

Uncertainty was the only certainty we knew. We lived in crisis mode, expecting and often getting, catastrophe at any moment. Eventually I found employment and left home every day, leaving behind children who desperately needed me to be with them, in order to receive a paycheck that did not support a family of seven.

I paid my tithing. I was temple-worthy. I prayed. And prayed. And prayed.

I did not deserve any of this.

My children were just that: children. They were innocent and wonderful.

They did not deserve any of this.

After all I could do, it was not enough to fix our world. And in the midst of all my efforts were my own imperfections and fears and distrust of life itself. I prayed and wept and pleaded with God.

Years of crisis upon catastrophe happened anyway. The trials did not disappear, they multiplied!

We did not deserve any of it.

There are people I love, including grandchildren, whose trials make my heart weep. Their only role in what has happened to them is that they lived. It crushes my heart to hear of their sorrows and griefs.

They do not deserve any of it.

This is what we deserve.

We have a Friend, our dearest Friend.

He suffered *all* things - - betrayal, rejection, gossip, rumors, lies, scourging, literally heart-breaking sorrow, and death, all these things and more - - only because He Lived.

He lived as Gods live, with Love in His Incomparable Heart.

He made Himself vulnerable, and kept Himself vulnerable, in Love.

Did He suffer because He deserved to suffer?

His life was Perfect. His life was Godly. In the midst of His Godly Life, did He have Un-Godly experiences?

No. He did not.

From His Life I learned that a Godly life is a life lived in Godly Love. A Godly Life has a heart willing to experience what *we* call *undeserved* pains and sorrows because Love is vulnerable. A Godly Life is acquainted with opportunities to practice what may be the Greatest of all Godly Attributes: *Forgiveness and Sacrifice.*

A God deserves, and wants, to be refined, growing Grace by Grace, in Godly love and Godly forgiveness, until that Godly Heart, moment by moment, has experienced the breadth and depth and scope of Eternal and Infinite Godhood - - Love that has no bounds, encompasses all things, overcoming all obstacles to Love.

A God deserves to be, and become, Godly.

I am a child of my Father in Heaven. I am His child and created to become Godly, as He is. I deserve to have a Savior and God who loves me, heals me, and makes a way for me to fulfill the purpose of my creation. I deserve to have someone who will love and forgive and provide a way for me live past my imperfections and become all I am meant and want to be: Perfect and Complete in my Godliness.

I deserve a life full of experiences, opportunities to become more perfect in the Godly Grace of Forgiveness. Following the example of my Savior, and with His help, I have been able to practice this great virtue

- - but only because I had opportunities to do so. I became able, over time, to forgive the man who betrayed our family so ruinously.

I deserve to become perfect in patient love. I am learning this slowly because there are some I love who still struggle to find their way in life. How else could I become like my Savior with His Infinite Patience if I did not have these experiences?

My children deserve these same opportunities. Their father deserves these same opportunities.

You deserve these same opportunities.

Jesus Christ deserved to fulfill the majesty of His Godhood, Perfect in every Loving Moment, Loving in every Perfect moment, and Complete in Experience of all Love. Every day of His mortality, culminating in Gethsemane and Golgotha, He did just that.

His Life was not unfair. And of all beings ever created and given Life . . .

He deserved it.

What a difference it makes to know this!

I *am* living the life that I deserve.

You are living the life you deserve.

We have the lives that Gods live, completing our Hearts in the Experience of Love. We are keeping company with our Friend and Savior.

We are doing what Gods do.

Our lives are not unfair.

We deserve this!

We are being schooled in Godhood!

Hearing Aids

I RECENTLY WATCHED A VIDEO titled *See The Amazing Moment When A Deaf Person Hears For The First Time.*[12]

As each person receives a hearing aid and hears for the first time their faces all have the same expression: Amazement.

Until that time they could see that others were speaking, but they could not understand the words. The words may have been words of comfort, but they could not be heard. Words of explanation, but not received. They could not know, of themselves, what was being said.

They were in many ways disconnected from friends, family, and their world.

Now modern medicine has found a way that doctors can help many people hear and understand friends and family and their world in a way they could never have imagined.

The gift of communication is a miracle we often take for granted.

There is another Physician, The Greatest Physician of all. He has promised us a Hearing Aid:

But the Comforter, which is the Holy Ghost, whom the Father will send in my name, he shall teach you all things, and bring all things to your remembrance, whatsoever I have said unto you.[13]

Our first Family and our first experience of Family Life were with our Heavenly Family, before we came to this Earth. Our first language was the Language of Heaven, the Language of Truth, the Language of Love. We are no longer home, we are for a time living in a boarding school. The languages spoken here are not our Native Language. Even though we do not remember our Heavenly Home, there is that Godly Child in us that yearns for Home, that wonders at the confusion of messages that bewilder us, and desires to hear the Truth and Love we inherently know must exist Somewhere.

Not hearing, knowing, and understanding the communications of Heaven can lead to a loneliness we don't understand and may not know how to ease. We are homesick for Heavenly Home Messages of Truth and Love

Our Father and Savior know this. They would comfort us and relieve our confusion. They would have us receive, understand, and know the Truths of our Heavenly Home, the Love They have for us. Moroni, a prophet of ancient times, promised:

> *And when ye shall receive these things [the Truths and Love of Heaven], I would exhort you that ye would ask God, the Eternal Father, in the name of Christ, if these things are not true; and if ye shall ask with a sincere heart, with real intent, having faith in Christ, he will manifest the truth of it unto you, by the power or the Holy Ghost.*
>
> *And by the power of the Holy Ghost ye may know the truth of all things.*[14]

And when your prayers are answered, and you hear these Truths and comprehend this Love, prepare to be Amazed.

Long-Suffering Love

THE SCRIPTURES TEACH THAT *CHARITY suffereth long . . . endureth all things . . . never faileth.*[15]

The Savior's Life and His Death were all about His Love for us and our redemption. He is the Perfect and Complete Example of patient, enduring, never-failing, *long-suffering* Love.

We also read that our Savior told His disciples to *Suffer the little children to come unto me, and forbid them not: for of such is the kingdom of God.*[16]

So I wonder, *What is long-suffering Love?*

I looked up the word Sufferance. And I learned that Sufferance is *consent or approval allowed by lack of interference or resistance; power or ability to withstand; see Patience.*[17]

Long-suffering Love is receiving others when they come to us. It is waiting a long time, enduring in patient Love, for them to come. And then receiving them, even when they are dirty after playing outside all day and we are completely clean.

The kingdom of God is full of God's children who come to Him, dirty and imperfect, and yet still we do come. The kingdom of God is full of people like me, who come and come again, who seek Him out and trust in His safe arms, His welcoming reception, His enduring willingness to receive us when we come - - however we come. His grateful gladness when we are finally there.

He suffers us to come, and suffered for us so that we can come in Hope and Safety. He endures the ups and downs of our journeys to Him. He never fails to believe in our ability to come to Him again and again until we are successful in staying with Him, in being like Him and One with Him, and our hearts never leave Him again.

I want to be like Him when I grow up. I am imperfect and practicing now. But some day my love will never fail, my heart will endure anything - everything - and I will Suffer long in receiving all God's children in my heart and my life.

I am relying on Him to Suffer me until that day.

A Star Wars Lesson in Guile

In *Star Wars*, Senator Palpatine, who is revealed as Darth Sidious, an evil Sith Lord, and who becomes Emperor, is a perfect example of guile in action. Using deceit and betrayal, he maneuvers himself into becoming Emperor. He promises freedom and delivers bondage. He develops a Death Star that annihilates an entire planet.

Anakin is beguiled by Palpatine's patient and carefully planned deceptions, which promise Anakin all that his heart desires while destroying the very things that he promises. Anakin becomes entirely bereft of all that he loves and Palpatine laughs as his nefarious purpose is accomplished. He clearly rejoices in the fruits of his malice.

Palpatine is a master of deception. He fakes compassion, interest, and friendship for Anakin, pretending to serve Anakin as he beguiles him into slavery. Rather than being Anakin's friend, his real design is to destroy Anakin and become his master. Watching Palpatine's methods is an instruction in the arts of Lucifer, the father of lies. Neither can be trusted.

The dictionary says that guile is to trick or deceive.

An essential attribute of the Savior is His Truth. In Him there is no deception, no hidden agenda.

He is open and blunt about His purpose, declared plainly in this way, *For behold, this is my work and my glory – to bring to pass the immortality and eternal life of man.*[18]

Jesus Christ lived and died and yet lives to serve us. His focus and intent is that our lives are filled with all the glory and blessings of God, and shows us the way to receive them. In addition, when Lucifer beguiles us down the road to destruction, Jesus Christ promises – and delivers – a way out.

He can be trusted. He is without guile, indeed.

In our journey to become even as He is, it is necessary for us to rid ourselves of all deceit and manipulation of others. Our relationships in life must be without hidden agendas; our sincere purpose should be to strengthen, encourage, and serve rather than belittle, mock, ridicule, discourage, enslave, or be served. To this end, as disciples of Christ we are required to keep the first two commandments: to love God and our fellow man. We must have integrity of heart.

Majestic and Godly of Heart, Jesus Christ is the Model, the Pattern, the Essence, of this Integrity. Eternally and forever He can be trusted to serve us. And as we follow Him we come closer to Godliness and all the blessings He has promised.

In Psalms it says, *Blessed is the man . . . in whose spirit there is no guile.*[19]

Blessed are those who associate with the Man who has no guile. As our hearts associate more closely to the great Heart of our Savior, we bless ourselves by that association. And in turn. those who associate with us are also blessed as we become trusted and trustworthy friends.

Do not give in to the dark side; Serve in the Love, Walk in the Light, of Truth.

Matter / Anti-Matter

ACCORDING TO PHYSICISTS, THERE EXISTS in the Universe matter and anti-matter. Symmetry magazine published an article that says, *Antimatter particles are almost identical to their matter counterparts except that they carry the opposite charge and spin. When antimatter meets matter, they immediately annihilate into energy.*

The article goes on to say:

Antimatter should have annihilated all of the matter in the universe after the big bang.

. . . the big bang should have created matter and antimatter in equal amounts. When matter and antimatter meet, they annihilate, leaving nothing but energy behind. So in principle, none of us should exist.

But we do. And as far as physics can tell, it's only because, in the end, there was one extra matter particle for every billion matter-antimatter pairs. Physicist are hard at work trying to explain this asymmetry.[20]

When someone treats us well, with kindness and respect, we feel like we matter.

In contrast, when we are ignored, neglected, or abused, we feel like we don't matter.

Matter/Antimatter physics is all about relationships.

Some people are like living antimatter, they ignore, mock, ridicule, abuse, and reject us. They seek to diminish and destroy the dignity and sanctity of others. When we are with them we are diminished. We know we *don't matter.* They have complete disregard for the sacredness of life.

Thankfully, there are those who enlarge mankind. They treat others with respect, kindness, appreciation. The receive us. They *attend* us. The dignity and sanctity of us all are protected by these kinds of people. They make us feel like we *matter.* They keep the sacredness of God's children alive.

Here is the Physics of God.

Jesus Christ is the One, in all the billions of antimatter people who may ever exist, He is the One who Matters above All of Us and ensures that we Matter, we exist, annihilation has been overcome and Life - - My Life and Your Life - - remains forever.

He is the Matter Particle by which we all survive.

He is the Matter Particle by which All was created.

Because of Him, We Matter.

P.S. According to Physicists, there is a particle called the God Particle. They don't know it yet, but that Particle is Jesus Christ. Because He Matters to make us Matter. I really know my stuff. Just sayin'.

The Virtue of Virtue

I HAVE BEEN THINKING ABOUT virtue, what it is, what it means. Then I read Matthew 5:13, *Ye are the salt of the earth: but if the salt have lost his savour, wherewith shall it be salted? it is thenceforth good for nothing, but to be cast out, and to be trodden under foot of men.*

Then I used my favorite verb and googled *salt* and *virtue* and found this:

> *On the fact of salt losing its virtue, cf. Thomson ('Land and the Book,' p. 382: 1887), "It is a well-known fact that the salt of this country [i.e. Palestine] when in contact with the ground, or exposed to rain and sun, does become insipid and useless. From the manner in which it is gathered [vide infra], much earth and other impurities are necessarily collected with it. Not a little of it is so impure that it cannot be used at all; and such salt soon effloresces and turns to dust - not to fruitful soil, however. It is not only good for nothing itself, but it actually destroys all fertility wherever it is thrown.... No man will allow it to be thrown on to his field, and the only place for it is the street; and there it is cast, to be trodden under foot of men.*[21]

Salt is used as a preservative in food. It is absolutely necessary for survival. Soldiers in Vietnam, a hot and humid place, were given salt tablets to help keep their body from dehydrating. Without it they often could not drink enough water to replace what they lost in the jungle heat.

Salt is used in cooking to enhance the flavors of other foods, bringing out the flavor of vegetables, meats, even some fruits. It is used in baking cookies and other sweet items. One web site for professional bakers says this about making good bread, *the role of salt is to enhance, and not take the place, of true bread flavor* and also this, *When salt is left out, the resulting dough is slack and sticky in texture, work-up is difficult, and bread volume is poor.*[22]

Salt also has some antiseptic and analgesic properties. A warm salt-water gargle is good for a sore throat. Many bacteria have a hard time living in a salt-concentrate.

Salt then, kept unsullied and unpolluted and used for the purpose for which it was created (maintaining its integrity and keeping its virtue), helps preserve life, prevent infections, restore health, enhances flavor and makes foods more palatable, and helps dough rise. The virtues of salt are intact when salt keeps its virtue.

Next, I looked up virtue in my *Merriam-Webster's Dictionary and Thesaurus.* One definition is this: *active power to accomplish a given effect: potency, efficacy.*

One synonym it gives for virtue is *integrity.* Integrity is being true to what you are, the purpose of your creation. When our feelings, thoughts, attitudes, desires, words, behavior, and actions are in harmony with what we are created to be . . . we have integrity.

That integrity gives us Virtue: active power to accomplish a given effect. We are potent in this world. We are efficacious.

When we maintain our integrity and keep our virtue, our efforts to be what our Lord asks us to be are effective. We are as salt and help preserve mortal and spiritual life as we help all we meet as we represent our Savior, His Truth and His Love. We help restore spiritual health. We enhance the flavor of others when they come to know who they really are through the eyes of their Lord. We make life more palatable for each other as we are true to our mandate: to love each other as our Lord loves us.

And we help each other rise to our purpose, meaning, and eternal potential.

However!

Ultimately, you and I will lose our savor somewhat. We are not perfect in maintaining our integrity and we occasionally lose some of our virtue. Is it irretrievably completely gone? Are we forsaken of all hope to regain our virtue and our savor?

No.

Because there is Another, of Perfect and Godly Virtue. As we turn to Him, repent, grow, heal, change, receive the effects of the Atonement . . . integrity is restored and virtue is redeemed.

Our Savior can renew our savor.

He is Virtue personified. His Virtue is Eternal, Infinite, Universal. It exists wherever He is. It exists when He is with us; it exists when we come to Him in need of forgiveness, purification, and healing.

He enhances our flavor; when we become bitter to ourselves He makes us palatable once more. He is healing antiseptic for our infected souls; He is comforting analgesic for our pain.

He is the Salt in the Bread of Life that causes it to rise, and rises to help us rise from whatever sunken depths we may have fallen.

He is the Bread itself.

He is the Salt Tablet in the heat of our jungles, lest we die of dehydration.

He is our Living Water.

Partake of His Salt, eat of His Bread, drink of His Water.

His Virtue will restore your Virtue.

I'm In Love And Always Will Be

I TURNED ON THE RADIO a long while ago and caught the last part of a song, and I had to google it as soon as possible. This is what I heard:

I will go down with this ship,
And I won't put my arms up and surrender.
There will be no white flag above my door.
I'm in love and always will be.[23]

I found out it was sung by Dido and went to Amazon and ordered the CD. Immediately.

Because from the very first it pierced my heart so deeply I could hardly breathe.

It's about me. And my kids. And I know the verses don't sound like a parenting song, and I don't care. The chorus is ALL about being the Mom.

Here's the thing: I'm *In Love*. And always will be.

My promise and commitment to my children is that I will always be *In* Love for them.

I will not go to another place. I will remain steadfast, IN Love. I will not move out of it, or wander. Love is the only place I will be.

And the One Promise I have made them, that I *WILL* keep, is this:

I will keep doing it wrong until I know how to do it right. I won't quit. Ever.

I can do this because my Father in Heaven gave me a place to stand, In Love, that is perfect - - with my imperfect Love I can stand there and refuse to be moved.

It is called the Atonement. He gave us a Savior so it would exist: this Amazing, Godly, Perfect, Marvelous, *Powerful* Place. For parents to stand.

Without the Atonement, parents have no place to go, no place to stand, for their children: no Place of Hope, no Place of Promise, no Place of Certainty, no Place of Saving Love. No Place of Redeeming Power.

We *need* that place as imperfect parents of imperfect children.

We need that place because without the Atonement, our ships, ALL our ships, would sink. And when we feel like our ship is still sinking, our Savior is on it with us, descending to our depths so we may rise.

And when our children feel they are on a sinking ship, we stand *In Love* with them, and the buoyancy of the Atonement, that Saving Place, saves the ship, our children, and us.

Our Father in Heaven needs that place, too. Because He, like us, has imperfect children. Born of His Perfect Parenting, He fashioned a Plan of Salvation and gave us a Savior and the Atonement so Father could stand firmly fixed in it and proclaim: *In this place is your Hope, your Promise, your Certainty, of Saving Love for you. It is the Place of Redemptive Power. Stand In this Love and Be Not Afraid. I am your Father. I'm In Love and Always will be.*

Jesus Christ is that Savior. He implemented that Atonement and that Place.

He did go down in the Ship of Exquisite Sorrow.

He did not put His arms up and surrender.

He raised no White Flag.

Standing, Kneeling, Suffering, Broken-Hearted - - In Love - - He gave Father, He gave us, He gave *me*, a place to stand.

So. Happy Father's Day . . .
Joyful Father's Day . . .
Thankful Father's Day . . .
To my Father and Savior, for giving me a place to stand and say to my children:

I'm In Love and Always will be.

All It Takes

THERE ARE MANY WORDS SPOKEN and written about what it means to be a disciple of Christ, a Follower of the Savior, a Christian.

I think it all comes down to some very simple principles.

Christ's purpose is to bring to pass the immortality and eternal life of man (this includes everyone).

His purpose from before the world was created was to be our Savior.

It is the essence of His very being.

If our purpose is to be like Him, then our purpose cannot be different than His.

The core of His purpose is that all mankind are healed of all things, including being a sinner. In other words, He desires that all are forgiven.

In that desire, the forgiveness of all resides in Christ and eagerly awaits the opportunity to dispense it to every penitent and repentant sinner.

He freely invites *ALL* to Come to Him and Receive.

There is *no one* that is Uninvited to Partake. His arms are stretched out still and wide open to all.

Forgiveness is in His heart, ready to be received by any and all who come to Him.

This healing mercy of forgiveness is born of the Godly . . . Perfect, Eternal, Infinite, Unending . . . Love He has for us all.

It is born of the Two Great Commandments:

He loves our Father.

He loves us.

Perfectly.

To be as He is, that is what we must do. Love well, establish forgiveness in our hearts, that healing mercy which we all need - every single one of us - and desire that all will turn to the Savior and the Atonement and receive it.

It is very simple. Books, thousands if not millions, have been written about this. It is what the scriptures are about. Words, uttered and written, are pleading for us to do these two things: Love God and Each Other.

It is the Law Of Godhood.

If we would be His disciples we *must* do this.

There is no room for revenge. There is no place for grudges. Neither unkindness, ridicule, mockery, scorn, nor sarcasm reside. There is no desire to belittle anyone.

There is only Godly Sorrow for the sinner and pleading, merciful, forgiveness.

Simple.

Very hard.

As in all things, the Heart of God will help our hearts to do this if we earnestly desire it.

And that is all it takes to be a Christian, a Follower, a Disciple.

A God.

Walking Point

MANY YEARS AGO I WAS talking with a Vietnam veteran who served in the infantry. He talked a bit about being on patrol and about the soldier who was walking point.

Walking point is the man at the front. His job is to watch for any sign of the enemy, mines, snipers, booby traps, anything that looks out of place - - any potential threat or danger.

He has to be alert. He must be aware. He must be entirely committed and focused on his responsibility and he must not get distracted.

If he is not good at what he needs to do, people will die.

It is the most dangerous position because whatever is there, the man walking point gets it first.

The purpose is to get safely through each patrol, through a jungle fraught with dangers, enemies, disease, and uncertainty. The goal is to overcome, endure, survive the tour of duty, and go home.

If the soldier walking point is good at what he does, he is the man to follow. He will keep you safe. He will get you home.

Recently I started thinking about this conversation and my Savior. And I realized something new.

All my life my Savior has been walking point for me. He has gone before. There is no threat or danger, no sniper or land mine or trip-wire or ambush that He does not see first, does not know intimately, and can not navigate His way safely through.

He is never deceived. He is never distracted. He has traveled this path, made this journey - all the way back Home - and He is never surprised or caught off guard.

If I am wounded, He has also been wounded on this Journey, and He knows how to heal me.

He knows how to get me safely Home no matter what obstacles are in my way.

If I step where He steps . . . I will get Home.

It doesn't matter what jungle or desert or stormy sea I encounter: He knows them all. He has traveled them all.

He knows the way, He *is* the Way, through everything.

If I walk in His footsteps, all the paths I must walk in this life: physical, emotional, mental, and spiritual - can be safely traveled.

If I step off the path, if I wander from His Way He goes after me, seeks me out, and guides me back. He knows the way back. Always. He forged it with His Body and Blood and Heart.

If I follow Him in my tour of duty, I will be safe, no matter what comes.

I will make it Home.

He is Walking Point for me.

Gollum, the Ring of Power, My Savior, and Me

I have been thinking about Power and Glory and Jesus Christ and me.

And for some reason, I started thinking of Gollum in *The Lord of the Rings*.

Gollum is called Smeagol before the Ring. One day Smeagol is fishing with his friend, Deagol, who finds the Ring in the river. Smeagol sees the Ring in his friend's hand and he wants it. And he kills his friend to get it.

He is willing to murder for the Ring before he ever has it. His choices make his heart ready for the Ring, to be its slave and desire no other master. He is a pitiful figure in that he is entirely the result of his own choices. Smeagol chooses a master who values him only as long as he is a useful slave.

Smeagol becomes so empty of everything but the Ring, he even loses his name. He becomes Gollum, always seeking to possess his Precious.

Instead, the Ring possesses him. It *owns* him. And he is never *Precious* to the ring.

A pitiable figure indeed.

An empty being. Empty of self.

The power of the Ring is power over others and it rules by fear. It is dangerous.

It is the Power of destruction; the Power of Death. Without glory.

What does this teach me about Power, Glory, my Savior, and me?

It is simple. The Power of my Savior is His Power over Himself: His thoughts, His words, His deeds . . . His Heart.

The Glory of the Savior is His Love for me. His Integrity of Heart. Armed with only the Power of His Love, He forges a path through Fear, Destruction, Slavery, and Death.

For me.

His commandments teach me the way to Glorious Power: Power over my Sacred Self. His will is that I have His same Glory, the Glory of Love and Serving others.

He never casts me off. If I stray from my Glory, from Him, He seeks me out. His only desire is to find me and love me back to my true self, my *full* self, and Him, that He may continue to help me enhance my personal Power, my personal Glory, with His Loving Guidance. He teaches me self-mastery - the source of His Power. He teaches me to Love and Serve: the source of His Glory.

His Power over me is the Power I give Him, because I love Him and seek His influence so I may be like Him. There is no fear in Him, no fear in me when I am with Him.

He is a Safe Place. Even when I stray.

With Him, I am never empty but always full.

He is my Power. I am His.

He is my Glory. I am His.

Not a Ring of Fear.

A Circle of Love.

Proginoskes, God, And Me

Sometimes when I am wondering about something, or maybe not wondering and thinking I already know, I am talking or writing about it and SUDDENLY!

Light!

And my eyes are opened. Literally. I can feel my eyes get big when it happens. Even though it is happening in my heart and mind - - my eyes are opened. And sometimes I want to laugh. Just because of the delightful joy of the whole thing. And sometimes it makes me cry, because of the incredible tenderness and gratitude of the whole thing. Or both.

Have you read Madeleine L'Engle's *Wind In the Door?* Proginoskes is a Namer. He knows the Names of all the stars. Meg asks Proginoskes how many stars there are.

Proginoskes answers, *What difference does it make? I know their names. I don't know how many there are. It's their names that matter.*[24]

I read this book decades ago and knew what I wanted to be when I grow up: a Namer.

When I learn something it feels like it is outlined in a precise, sharp line of Light. Like a pen and ink drawing, but the ink is Light. And I see it in an exact way. Uncomplicated. Standing alone, just as it is. It settles in me and fits. It belongs to me. It is peaceful. It is beautiful!

It is Named. No longer unknown or equivocal.

The Holy Ghost does that. And then He lets us in on it. He does that with and for us.

I think the Holy Ghost is a Namer.

I do fear the unknown. Things that I don't understand and don't make sense. Things that don't have a name. I don't know how to know them. I can't incorporate them. They don't fit. And often the problem is that there are people who are saying, *This is the name of this thing. It is your fault. You are not good. You are ugly. You are bad. You are not lovable. You cannot do it. You don't matter. God is done with you. This is the truth about this thing.*

It feels dark. It does not fit inside and I can't find me in it or it in me. It does not belong. I am lost. There is no peace. It is ugly.

It is a lie, but I can't find where it is false, so I believe it anyway. And it leaves me even more fearful and more unknowing. Because, believing I know and understand, I do not seek further and the Truth is even more Unknown because I am not seeking it.

Oh, those are dark times! Sometimes they last for years.

When I finally hear the true Name I am in Light. It is brilliant. It is comforting. It is God. And it settles right in and fits me. It belongs as if it was there before and suddenly discovered. The blanket of darkness was just removed and the Named Truth uncovered.

The shadow is gone and the fear with it.

And I have learned that true Names are always given in Love, and that Love casts out fear.

Even when the circumstances do not change, the Love changes everything.

I can endure. Whatever the Name of the situation before me, that Name also means I am not alone and I can endure.

I am often told, as a comfort, that my Father knows my Name. The comfort is that I am not part of a Generality, a member of a group called Children. I am singular, specific, uniquely Known. My Father sees me individually. I matter personally to Him.

How necessary, critically important, that I also know my Father's Name.

How vital to my Joy and my Peace and my knowledge of ME for me to know Him!

Without His True Name I am unable to know myself completely. I am even unable to know you and your True Name.

The True Name of my Father eradicates all mysteries. There are no Unknowns. Nothing to Fear.

Father and I? We are Twins and He does not keep secrets from me. (I know as I write this that these things are true). He reveals True Names as soon as my heart is ready to comprehend.

So I know He is faithful to me. And I want to be faithful to Him, because He needs good friends and I want to be one of them. I don't want Him to be lonely and miss me! And I don't want others to be lonely and miss *Him*, either. So I try to Name Him as much as I can.

His Name is Safe. His Name is Restorer. His Name is Love. His Name is Compassion. His Name is Forgiveness. His Name is Joy and Sorrow and Lonely and Magnificent.

His Name is my name. His Name is your name. We are His children and we are Twins.

I am a Namer. I know this is true. I know this is *Truth*.

I am not always true to my Name. When I sin it is like having spiritual amnesia. I forget who I am.

Thank God, TRULY thank God - both Father and Son - that there is an Atonement that keeps my Name for me and I can remember and know myself again. I matter. I am found.

Oh, Thank God!

Tears of gratitude for the Tenderness of the whole thing. And the Joy. And the Light.

Father could tell me how many children He has. But it doesn't matter. He knows my Name.

And I know His.

Until the Whistle Blows

OKAY, WE'RE TALKING FOOTBALL HERE. Just so you know.

Nebraska was winning. They had a 29-game winning streak for season opener games. That changed when they played BYU. People are calling it the *Mangum Miracle at Memorial*. It happened September 5, 2015, when BYU played the Nebraska Cornhuskers in Lincoln, Nebraska, at their Memorial Stadium.

BYU had lost their starting quarterback, Taysom Hill. They found out later he was done for the season. So, BYU had Tanner Mangum on the field. It was Tanner Mangum's first college football game. The team was trying to pull out a win.

The game's not over until the whistle blows. They had one second left on the clock. It looked impossible. BYU kept playing anyway. Tanner threw a 42-yard pass to Mitch Matthews. Mitch caught it for a touchdown. The whistle blew. The final score was BYU 33, Nebraska 28.

Some sports writers don't say that Tanner threw a football. He threw a prayer.

Why am I telling you this?

When I was five years old I remember thinking about suicide for the first time. In the 63 years I have lived since then, there have been many times when it has crossed my mind. It sometimes stays there and settles in for a while. Being here is very hard when you think you can't do it, you are only getting it wrong. I mean, it is *very hard*.

So I am talking to those who are struggling with being here. And those who are struggling to help someone who is struggling with being here.

And here is what I have to say.

First: The game is not over until the whistle blows. You do not have the whistle. You don't get to choose. The game may seem to last an unconscionably long time. That's okay. The Timekeeper is your Father in Heaven. He knows just how long you need to play. He also knows that you can win your game. The whistle will blow when the time is right. You can trust Him in this.

So! Don't Quit! Stay on the field. Stay in the Game.

Until the Whistle Blows.

Second: You are not alone on the field. Tanner did not win the game by himself. Mitch did not win the game by himself. All the players blocking and making way for the quarterback to be able to throw, and the receiver to catch, the ball . . . it took every single player to win the game.

You have a Team of Angels on your side. I promise.

Jesus Christ is your Coach and He *never* leaves the field until the whistle blows.

When you think you can't do it any longer, remember: Jesus Christ, the Angels of Heaven, and your Earthly team (Yes! You have them, even if you don't know it or can't feel or remember it!) are all on the field with you.

Until the Whistle Blows.

Third: THROW A PRAYER!

This is what it sounds like or looks like.

God, help me!

Keep breathing.

Get a blessing.

Keep breathing.

A Miracle will happen, the Greatest Miracle Ever! It's this: You find yourself able to stay in the game until the Whistle Blows.

So Keep Breathing. Throw a Prayer.
Until the Whistle Blows.

In this life, unlike Football - - the Coach is on the Field ALL THE TIME!
ALL the Time!

That is why He came here in the first place.

That is what the Atonement is all about.

So. Remember.

You are not alone on the field. Ever. Remember 2 Kings 6:16? *And he answered, Fear not: for they that be with us are more than they that be with them.* You have more people on your team helping you than there are adversaries, trying to block your way. I know this.

Trust your Father in Heaven. He is the Timekeeper. He has the Whistle.

Jesus Christ is the Coach. He never leaves the field. He is there Until the Whistle Blows.

Throw a Prayer.

Keep Breathing.

Until the Whistle Blows.

Love Will Keep Us Alive

THE EAGLES SING A SONG with a chorus that goes like this:

Lost and lonely
Now you've given me the will to survive
When we're hungry
Love will keep us alive[25]

And a big grin spread over my face. I am 68 years old and I know that you can starve to death if you don't have food to eat for an extended period of time. And no matter how much two people love each other, you can't eat love.

So why was I grinning? Because this is a True Love Song. And the Eagles are right, Love Will Keep Us Alive.

We are more than these mortal bodies we wear while we sojourn upon this Earth. We had Life before this Mortal Existence. We will have Life after it. We are now in School, the School of the Gods. We are having experiences, often called Trials. We are Students, imperfect children of a Perfect God, practicing Godhood.

We are often Hungry. We Hunger for Spiritual Food, we Hunger for Home, we Hunger for Connections, Light, Truth, Meaning. We Hunger for Hope - - that these experiences have purpose, our pains, discouragement, and fears have meaning. We Hunger to know we will not

Fail - - even as we falter, we Hunger for Forgiveness and the chance to go forward and succeed

We are desperately Hungry for the reassurance that we are not doing this alone. Because we know we can't.

Before All Things - - this Earth, Life, Planets, Sun, Moon, Stars - - Before All Things that in them are - - was Father. With a Plan. The answer to our fears, failures, mistakes, loneliness, homelessness, trials, and hunger.

The Answer is Jesus Christ. The Answer is a Savior. A Redeemer. A Friend. The Answer is the Atonement. The Answer is Hope, Purpose, Meaning, Connections, Home.

The Answer is Love. The Charity of God.

That is what Mortal Life and this Earth are all about.

Everywhere I look I see someone who is Hungry. It may be myself. It is assuredly others. I can guarantee it is Everyone at various times in their lives.

As a disciple of Christ, I can offer the Love I feel from my Savior and help someone else Survive. And others do the same for me.

Why was I grinning? Because I know this one true thing about my Savior:

Lost and lonely
Now He's given me the will to survive
When we're hungry
His Love Will Keep Us Alive.

Tongues of Charity

THE GIFT OF TONGUES IS mentioned several times in the scriptures. In Acts we are told, *And they were all filled with the Holy Ghost, and began to speak with other tongues, as the Spirit gave them utterance.*[26] There are many scriptures[27] that tell us that the gift of tongues, or speaking in a language not previously known to you, is a gift of the Spirit. Its purpose is to bring us to Christ and His Truth.

Here is the first principle of the first discussion that missionaries teach to all, the center and core of all Truth:

We are children of a Father God Who loves us. He has provided a Savior Who will bring us Home to live with our Father in joy and peace forever - - if we will come to Christ and follow Him.

If the gift of tongues is a spiritual gift, a manifestation of the Holy Ghost working in us, it follows that the only words we can speak under that influence are words of Love and Truth. It is not a gift that will manifest in criticism, sarcasm, ridicule, anger, mockery, or condemnation. We will not speak to humiliate, embarrass, diminish, or belittle others. No heart comes to Christ's Truth and Love by that language.

So why is it that, having the Gift of the Holy Ghost, we do not eschew the tongues of the world and speak in other new Heavenly Tongues every time we open our mouths? Tongues that affirm value, love, respect, dignity, friendship, and Godly Parentage? Tongues that entreat us to come to Christ and Live?

What a blessed place would be our homes, neighborhoods, communities, work and schools, our church congregations, if we *were all filled with the Holy Ghost, and began to speak with other tongues, as the Spirit gave [us] utterance* . . . .

Tongues of Charity.

The Conquering Hero and King

WHEN THE SAVIOR CAME TO this Earth, He was not the Messiah the Jews expected. They looked for a Conquering Hero, One who would be their Earthly King and deliver them from Roman bondage and all other enemies. He would rule to their advantage in all things.

Instead, He came as Humble Teacher, a Meek Messiah whom many could not recognize or accept. He presented more as Servant than Ruler. He came in the Power of Truth rather than the power of the Sword.

Not what they expected or wanted.

We read and wonder, *How could they not know?* They had centuries of prophets and prophecies that told them exactly Who He was and what to expect of Him.

How marvelous that we have the fullness of the gospel, living prophets again in our day, ordinances, saving covenants, the Gift of the Holy Ghost, and scriptures at hand! We have all we need to know and recognize our Savior, Deliverer, and King!

And yet, sometimes we are like the Jews of the New Testament. We say that Christ has come to suffer so that we may not have to suffer as He did. So when we suffer, and we assuredly do - repeatedly - we wonder, *Where is God?*

He may be attending, strengthening, and comforting us - - but sometimes we begin to doubt Him because what we want is to be delivered from the trials before us. We want Him to make the hard things go away. We may even doubt the gospel, the church leaders, our promised blessings.

We may criticize and even become bitter towards all we are taught and finally, even bitter towards God.

We begin to disbelieve that He is our Messiah, because He is not blessing us the way we expect.

Sometimes we don't want His miracles of strength and endurance. We don't want a God strengthening us to become Godly, too.

We want a magician with a magic wand or spell that causes our heartaches and hardships to disappear.

The purpose of the Savior is to overcome the obstacles of death and damnation. He shows the way so we may continue our journey to our own Godly exaltation.

The experiences on our journeys are the necessary Forge of Godhood.

If He takes them away, His purpose is naught and our journeys are pointless.

He came to succor us in our infirmities, not to deny us the mortal experiences that are necessary for us in our Godly becoming. And we do *not* suffer as He suffered - - the depths and torments of Hell to free us all from the bondage of our sins. He is our Deliverer from eternal condemnation. We suffer a broken heart and contrite spirit for the sorrow of our own sins, and that sorrow only, to take us to the Messiah who paid the rest of the price in the Garden with a Godly Sorrow, a Godly Contrition, a broken Godly Heart,

The next time we begin to doubt that He is delivering us . . . we may need to remember that He is the Conquering Hero of Gethsemane and Golgotha, and He is the King of Comfort and Strength. He is the God of the Miracle of Endurance.

He *is* the awaited Messiah.

The Prodigal's Brother

THE *TRUE* STORY OF THE Prodigal Son casts the Prodigal's Brother in a very different Light. His role is vital to the story's existence and the return of every wayward child. Without the Brother, there is no story to tell.

In the parable, the father waits for his wayward son and watches for him constantly.

The Truth is, the Father sends His Elder Son to bring home the lost and rebellious child. The Father commissions the Son to create a Path and make the Way of Homecoming and Reconciliation.

The Beloved Elder Son does this and seeks each lost brother or sister and entreats them to return. He does not cease to do this, as the Father does not cease to Watch for their return. They Slumber not, nor Sleep.

As the Prodigal is found, the Brother entreats him to come home. There is a Price that must be paid to free the wandering child from the Wicked Master he has served. The Elder Son pays the price every time.

The Father, Who still watches unceasingly, sees afar off that His Children are returning Home. And always there are Two Who return, for no Lost Child ever returns without the help of the Brother.

Great is the Joy and Celebration of the Father and the Brother over the return of him who was lost.

The Feast is attended by All!

The Father's Heart is Full of Thanksgiving for the return of the Prodigal Son.

The Elder Son is the Father's Eternal Hope for all His children who Wander. The Father's Heart gives the Brother all Recognition for returning another child, who is Lost no more.

And Wondrous Indeed is the Heart of the Brother.

(Note: The Feast serves a Fatted Lamb - - it symbolizes the Brother who was slain as Ransom for each child. It is the Sacrifice of which we all must partake to Return Home.)

A Godly Life

I HAVE BEEN THINKING FOR a long time about what it means to live a Godly Life. I watch, read about, and think of my Father in Heaven and my Savior and I want to be like Them. As the years have passed I have come to know what that really means.

My Father has children who have strayed. Some strayed before the Earth was even created and were denied their birthright and all that goes with it. Some came to Earth and did not faithfully endure this mortal experience. Some falter and do not give up. They continue to press forward in Christ and they persevere.

Father is living a Godly Life.

I know many, myself included, who struggle with children who wander.

We are living Godly Lives.

My Father, understanding before His children were born that we would waver, stray, be lost, sin . . . prepared His Heart to Love us Everlastingly, Eternally, Infinitely. He is not deterred in His Integrity of Love. His Heart is fixed and He has a plan whereby all can be saved. Rather than hide His Heart in shame, He boldly announces to the Universe a Plan of Salvation, a Savior, an Atonement . . . all because of His great love for His wayward children.

Father is living a Godly Life!

There are many on this Earth who love with immovable hearts. We do not yield to doubts, anger, fear, shame, or scorn. We point to that same Plan, Savior, Atonement and boldly endure in love.

We are living Godly Lives.

Jesus Christ, our Savior, and Father's Beloved Son, loved our Father and us so *entirely* that He dedicated His Eternal Purpose to Save us all, giving Father the Salvation that only Jesus could promise and provide. He did not scorn Father for His imperfect children, but rather embraced Father's Parental Heart and gave Succor and Hope where before was only condemnation and death.

Jesus Christ is living a Godly Life.

There are many of us who rise up as friends, encourage the wandering child and suffering parent, and remind them of Hope, the Eternal and Infinite nature of the Atonement, and declare they are not alone in their love.

We are living Godly Lives.

When Lehi partook of the Fruit of the Tree, which is the Love of God, the Gospel of Jesus Christ, the Atonement, even Christ Himself - - he had two sons who would not come and partake. There was a great and spacious building filled with those who mocked and spoke in derision to those who were partaking of the fruit.

When I see the sorrows, anguish, and isolation of those who are living Godly Lives of Hope and Sorrow and Suffering and Endurance for loved souls who have lost their way . . . I wonder. Did those people in the building, pointing fingers of mockery and ridicule, scorn Lehi for having sons who strayed entirely from the path to the Tree of Love and Life? Did they taunt, judge, and condemn *him* for not being *good enough* to get Laman and Lemuel to partake?

How would we treat Father if He lived in our neighborhood and we watched His fallen children leave home and not return for years . . . or ever? Would we treat Him with disdain? Would we jeer and gossip as He lived His Godly Life?

Or would we be like the Savior, and Honor the Father for His unwavering Heart?

The Savior came here to show us how to live a Godly Life. He did not come here to save us from having to live a Godly Life. Godly Lives are not lived in a perfect world with perfect people. Godly Lives are lived in imperfect worlds with imperfect people. They are the Lives that Father and our Savior live *all the time!*

Godly lives are about how our Hearts respond to imperfections.

Thanking my Father and Savior for showing me the Way.

So grateful for Godly Lives.

Sidekicks

MY GRANDSON WROTE AN EMAIL this year about the words of Genesis 2:18, *And the Lord God said, it is not good that the man should be alone; I will make him an help meet for him.* (I looked up *help meet* and it means a companion or partner.)

My grandson and his companion noticed that missionaries are sent out in pairs, as are home teachers and visiting teachers. Relief Society presidents, Elders Quorum presidents, Bishops, and any other head of an organization, have counselors. President Monson has two counselors. No one has to do their job alone.

As I read his email, my mind took a left turn and I started thinking about the Lone Ranger. My grandfather never missed an episode. The radio (a piece of furniture taller than I), was beside his kitchen table. He was hard of hearing so he sat, with a glass of milk and his Hi Ho crackers, directly in front of the radio to listen to his episodes. He also listened to the Cisco Kid. And at night, if I was quiet and my parents thought I was asleep (so they forgot to turn down the radio), I listened to Roy Rogers.

Besides being Westerns, what did these programs have in common?

The hero had a sidekick.

The Lone Ranger had Tonto. The Cisco Kid had Pancho. Roy Rogers had Pat Brady.

Then I started thinking about the Lord of the Rings, (the books, not the movies). Frodo had Sam. And I thought about Star Wars, how Han Solo has Chewie.

I thought about how David had Jonathan. I *love* Jonathan!

Then I thought about how Joseph Smith had his brother, Hyrum. Which makes me weep. (Hyrum is one of my favorite people ever. I want to hug him good when I see him again.)

I realized that the scripture is about sidekicks.

And I saw how each of us has the thing that only we can do. Frodo, Joseph Smith, David - - each of us lives a life that has individual purpose, personal tasks, trials, and challenges which we must endure.

We each have an heroic purpose to fulfill.

Which of course made me think of my Savior. And of Gethsemane.

And I remembered that an angel was sent to administer to Him, to strengthen and encourage Him to endure a task that only He could endure and complete.

An angelic sidekick.

And I realized what a Heavenly assignment it is to be walking the Earth and be a sidekick. And I saw how critical it is that our eyes and hearts are open to the person in our path, because they are on their own heroic journey, and in the moment that our paths cross they may need our attendance. They may need the smile, the look, the nod, the hug, the reaching out that says, *I see you. You can do this. You are doing well. Don't give up!*

Then I thought of the baptismal covenant, wherein we promise to bear one another's burdens, mourn with those that mourn, comfort those that stand in need of comfort, and to be a witness of God always - - which would mean that we would be a witness of God's love always.

Guess what? We covenant to be sidekicks.

And what does God promise to give us when we make that covenant? The Gift of the Holy Ghost! A Master Sidekick! He does ALL this stuff! We can't fail at this because we have a Godly Expert on the Sidekick thing!

So I think some more. What if being a Sidekick is actually the most Epically Heroic Act in the Eternity of the Universe? What if the Sidekick *is* the Hero?

What if supporting someone else in their own personal success is the best thing you can do with your life?

Which takes me back to the Savior. And Gethsemane.

Yup. The culminating Best Thing He did with His life was give it - so I can succeed.

He is my Sidekick. He helps me get up when I fall. Because of His Heroic Hour, I can have my Heroic Hour. His support, encouragement, and strength are Infinite and Eternal. For me. And for you. An Help Meet.

And I realize that when we do our Best Things, we are His sidekicks, too. Helping Him help us. Sidekicks helping Sidekicks. Help Meets all around. A Circle. Love that!

How I LOVE my Help Meet, Hero, Sidekick, and Savior.

One With God . . .

IF:

Father makes only Godly choices, He is a God,
And
Jesus Christ makes only Godly choices, He is a God,
Then
Jesus Christ = Father
And They are Twins = One

Therefore - - If:

We make only Godly choices, we are Gods,
Then
We = Jesus Christ = Father
And We are All Twins = One

(Bear in mind, that making only Godly choices begins with what we choose to love . . . it starts in the heart - - which would make a GREAT song title and I think I will work on it!)

(And please note that this would answer our Savior's prayer when He prayed for us to be One as He and the Father are One.[28] Our Hearts would be One with Theirs. Think about it.)

It Starts in the Heart

It starts in the Heart
And spreads out from there;
It goes to your toes and
The ends of your hair.

Your lips speak His words,
Your smile lingers.
Your eyes will light up as it
Goes to your fingers.

You can't help yourself,
You start acting like Him,
Your body's an anthem
And singing a Hymn

That starts in the Heart!

So if you want to know Him,
His love to impart -
If you want to be Him
It starts in your Heart!

And you'll be an anthem
Singing your part - -
The music Celestial
That starts in your Heart!

Celestial Math

SOMETIMES I WRESTLE WITH PROBLEMS until I am exhausted, discouraged, and hopeless. I keep coming up with the same answer - and it just makes my problem bigger. So the answer is not a solution - it's a bigger problem!

Sheesh, guys!

And then today I saw it all in a brand new way.

Let's say I am trying to solve this math problem: $2 + 3$. The answer is 5. A no-brainer.

I take my paper to the teacher and she tells me it's wrong. I do it again. Same answer.

Finally, I ask the teacher for help.

She tells me I copied it wrong, and shows me the real problem.

The real problem is $2 + 3 + 10$. The answer is 15.

I couldn't solve the problem because I didn't know what it was. I was in too big a hurry to look at the whole thing.

I try to solve another problem. It is $3 + 7 + 10$. The answer is 20. Another no-brainer.

I take my paper to the teacher and she tells me it's wrong! I do it again. Same answer.

Finally, I ask the teacher for help.

She tells me I copied it wrong and shows me the real problem.

The real problem is $7 + 10$. The answer is 17.

I couldn't solve the problem because I didn't know what it was. I made it bigger than it really was.

Sometimes in Life I get so terribly discouraged because I am trying to solve a problem and I can't. No matter how hard I try. No matter what I do.

Finally, I humble myself and ask for Heavenly Help.

Celestial Math Tutor to the Rescue! Cape and everything!

I am told I left out some important information. Or I am told that I am making it much harder than it is because I am adding extra stuff that is not mine to solve - - I am trying to solve someone else's homework! (And often, the homework I am trying to do is God's! No wonder I don't get anywhere!)

And what seemed a complicated mess is now made plain. And solvable.*

The Celestial Math Lab is ALWAYS open!

Trust the Tutor!

Jesus Christ *is* the Eternal Solution in the Math Lab of Life!

---

* *Sometimes I want the solution to be that the problem is removed. When I am humble I often find out that the solution is to stay close to the Tutor so I can endure the situation that faces me.*

Best Love Song EVER!

Johnny Mathis sings:

> *When I am with you I am nothing I was before*
> *I am everything I ever wished I could be and more*
> *So it's not just for what you are yourself that I love you as I do*
> *But for what I am when I am with you.*[29]

By the time my Savior is through with me, I hope to be *everything I ever wished I could be and more.*

It won't be His fault if I'm not.

And when I am with Him, I believe it will happen.

And *Herein is Love* - - He gives us the *Capacity to Live* as we are meant to *Be.*

So, Dearest Savior,

> *it's not just for what You are yourself that I love You as I do*
> *But for what I am when I am with You.*

(When we are like Him, other people are liking who they are when they are with us. Think about it. Therein is our love, keeping the two Great Commandments. Pretty Cool. We would be Twins with Heaven.)

ENDNOTES

1. 1 John 3:10

2. http://www.goodnewshalifax.com/MoreGoodNews/Good
    NewsinRealLife/ChileMineRescue/tabid/371/language/en-US/
    Default.aspx

3. John 8:11

4. Isaiah 1:18

5. 2 Corinthians 7:10

6. Alma 7:11-13

7. 2 Nephi 26:25

8. Matthew 11:28

9. Matthew 11:28-30

10. Mark 4:39

11. Mosiah 18:9

12. http://www.huffingtonpost.com/2015/02/10/people-hear-for-first-
    time-video_n_6646594.html

13. John 14:26

14. Moroni 10:4-5

15. 1 Corinthians 13:4, 8

16. Mark 10:14

17. Webster's Ninth New Collegiate Dictionary

18. Moses 1:39

19. Psalms 32:2

20. Kwon, Diana. Ten things you might not know about antimatter. *Symmetry* April 2015. http://www.symmetrymagazine.org/article/april-2015/ten-things-you-might-not-know-about-antimatter

21. Pulpit Commentary. http://biblehub.com/matthew/5-13.htm

22. http://www.kingarthurflour.com/professional/salt.html

23. Dido Armstrong, Rollo Armstrong and Rick Nowels 2003 *White Flag* sung by Dido

24. L' Engle, Madeleine. Wind In The Door.

25. Vale, Peter, Jim Capaldi, and Paul Carrack. *Love Will Keep Us Alive* sung by the Eagles.

26. Acts 2:4

27. 1 Corinthians 12:10; Omni 1:25; Moroni 10:15; Doctrine and Covenants 46:24.

28. John 17:21

29. Al Stillman, Benjamin Weisman Lyrics © Warner/Chappel Inc., Music Sales Corporation "When I Am With You Lyrics." Lyrics.com. STANDS4 LLC, 2018. Web. 25 Jan. 2018. <https://www.lyrics.com/lyric/1990531>.

Made in the USA
Las Vegas, NV
24 February 2021